Up and Running in 30 Days

Make Money Your First Month in Real Estate

Carla Cross, CRB

Real Estate
Education Company
a division of Dearborn Financial Publishing, Inc.

Acquisitions Editor: Christine E. Litavsky
Managing Editor: Jack Kiburz
Editorial Assistant: Stephanie C. Schmidt
Interior Design: Professional Resources & Communications, Inc.
Cover Design: Salvatore Concialdi

Published by Real Estate Education Company,
a division of Dearborn Financial Publishing, Inc.

Library of Congress Cataloging-in-Publication Data

Cross, Carla
    Up and running in 30 days: make money your first month in real estate / Carla Cross.
      p.   cm.
    Includes bibliographical references and index.
    ISBN 0-7931-1348-2
    1. Real estate agents—United States. 2. Real estate business—United States—Marketing.
I. Title. II. Title: Up and running in thirty days.
HD278.C76 1995   95-2149
333.33'068'8—dc20   CIP

Acknowledgments

Up and Running in 30 Days has evolved from the experiences and feedback of new agents who have helped me refine this program, both at my first real estate office and at my current Windermere Real Estate–West Seattle office. Special thanks and gratitude go to staff advisers Mike Donaldson, Lisa Mundahl, Tim Smallwood, Norma Jean Mortensen, Scott Monroe and Bob Byrne. Serving as advisers to our new agents, these pros have dedicated themselves and their invaluable expertise to this program. The synergy generated by these exceptional REALTORS® is inspiring to everyone in our office.

—Carla Cross

Contents

Preface

Up and Running in 30 Days is dedicated to all the agents who have taught me "what works." I have enjoyed helping great salespeople launch their careers to high profitability—quickly. The purpose of *Up and Running* is to help *you* do the same.

In *Up and Running* you have a personal, detailed, workable business-developing plan. It has taken me two decades of real estate sales, management and training work to organize and prioritize this business—so that you won't have to!

With *Up and Running*, you can start your career today, using the same activities top producers use to create multimillion-dollar careers. Congratulations on choosing to become a dedicated, professional, successful salesperson. Before you know it, you will be serving as a success story for the industry!

Introduction

This business planning system for the new agent will ensure you a *quick, successful start* in the business. The plan will also help you to build *success habits* that will set the pace for your entire career. In *Up and Running* you will find:

- the business-developing plan followed by top agents;
- the concepts behind the plan, so that you can adapt the plan to meet your needs;
- a framework for a business plan for each week of your first four weeks in the business;
- the support and technical activities you should be doing your first four weeks; and
- sales skills, including specific scripts.

The biggest reason agents fail is that, at the beginning of their career, they created the wrong business plan. That is, their daily *activities* did not bring them the quick money that they had thought they could make in real estate. *This book provides a proven business plan to get you where you want to go—at least one sale in your first 30 days in the business.*

To help you create your business plan, included in *Up and Running* are:

- a full set of planning guidelines,
- a sample business development plan,
- business-producing assignments,
- assignments for business support,
- a manager/facilitator checklist, and
- audiotapes for sales skill development.

In short, the *what, how, why, how much, when and where* of real estate sales.

Up and Running is on based on two unique foundations:

1. *30 Days to Dollars*—the activity plan for success
2. Seven Critical Sales Skills for success

When you start your real estate career, you will probably receive lots of information, which will need to be prioritized. Unfortunately, new agents have no basis for deciding which information is most important. *Up and Running* is organized to ensure your success. In this planning system, information is prioritized under two categories:

1. Business-producing activities, *or*
2. Business-supporting activities

Guess which activities unsuccessful agents overinvest their time in? That's right. Business-supporting activities. As you follow the guidelines in this system, you will naturally set your schedule toward the right prioritization of activities—and *fast success*.

The Five Principles of a High-Producing Business

Too often new agents receive an activity plan without an explanation of the principles behind the plan. To get your business off to a fast start and keep it on track for the long term, you need to understand and apply the *five principles of creating a high-producing business*:

1. Start the business cycle by talking to people.

2. Stay on the business path.

3. Prioritize your activities.

4. Prospect like the pros.

5. Work the numbers.

Figure 1.1   Business Cycle

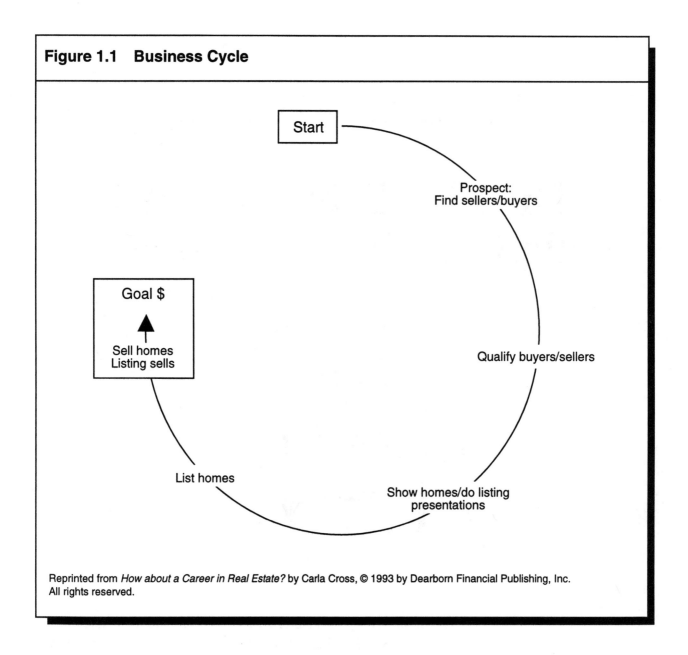

Principle One: Start the Business Cycle

The most important principle in the activity plan is this: Business starts when you start talking to people.

> "... *the only message that needs to be stressed is to prospect a major portion of your day. Get the scripts and dialogues needed to cold call, door knock, work expireds and FSBOs. Do the work, and you'll become a great, consistently high-producing agent.*"
>
> **—Rick Franz, third-year top-producing agent**

To be successful quickly, the most important activity you need to accomplish every day—at least *four hours a day*—is to *talk to people to get a lead.* This activity starts the business cycle (see Figure 1.1).

The more times you talk to people, the greater your chances to continue the business cycle, to work with and sell someone a property. *Up and Running* will ensure that you spend enough time in the sales cycle to reach your monetary expectations.

Principle Two: Stay on the Business Path

> *"If you don't prospect, the potential for failing in this business greatly increases. I wish I knew how to tell other agents, in a nice way, to get the hell out of my way when they try to discourage me from proactive prospecting!"*
>
> **—Brian Orvis, first-year, top-producing agent**

Your objective in real estate sales is to get on the *business path* and to stay on it every day until you get to the end of the road—a sale or a listing sold. Figure 1.2 illustrates the business path.

Seems simple, doesn't it? However, many obstacles get in the way—anxiety over making sales calls, fear of not knowing enough, dread of rejection, need to be more organized, quest for more knowledge—the list is endless. *Up and Running* will help you to stay on the business path, while filling some of those other needs in the correct relationship to your mission—which is to *sell real estate.*

Principle Three: Prioritize Your Activities

> *"What I would have given to have had a job description indicating a plan of attack. For example, this is how your day must be scheduled: prospecting three hours, follow-up, clerical, etc."*
>
> **—Rick Franz, now a very successful agent,**
> **formerly in hotel management**

It's all here, Rick, in *Up and Running*—the hours, the prioritizations and the concepts behind the schedule. First and foremost, you must spend at least four hours a day starting the sales cycle. But where do the other activities fit in? To teach the habits of successful agents, this system has

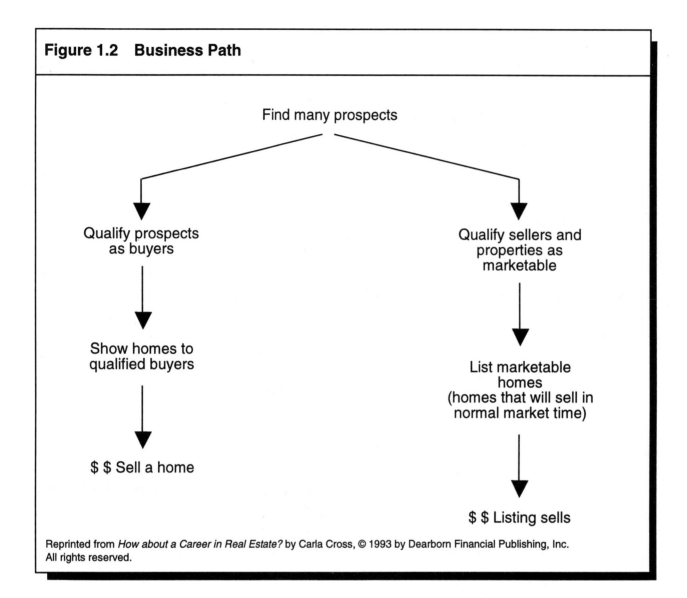

Figure 1.2 Business Path

Find many prospects

Qualify prospects
as buyers

Qualify sellers and
properties as
marketable

Show homes to
qualified buyers

List marketable
homes
(homes that will sell in
normal market time)

$ $ Sell a home

$ $ Listing sells

been prioritized for you. As you plan each day, you'll see that your activities will fall under two categories:

1. ***Business Development*** (activities in the sales cycle)
   - Contacting prospects
   - Following up on leads
   - Qualifying buyers
   - Showing homes to qualified prospects
   - Writing and presenting offers to purchase
   - Giving listing presentations to qualified sellers
   - Listing marketable properties
   - Attending offer presentations on your listings

Figure 1.3   Prototype Schedule

Time Commitments: How to allocate your time to ensure quick success.

Activity	Daily	No./Week	Hours
Business development plan	4 hours	5 days	20
Open house		Once a week	3–4
Floor time		1 day	3
Business meeting	1 hour	Once a week	1
Office education	1 hour	1 day	1
Mgr/agent counseling		Once a week	1–2
Previewing	2 hours	5 days	10

Schedule

Mon.	8:00 – 8:45	Meet with manager
		Paperwork/calls
	8:45 – 9:30	Business meeting
	9:30 – 12:30	New office lising tour
	Lunch	
	1:30 – 5:30	Business plan
Tues.	Day off	
	Take it!!	
Wed.	8:00 – 9:00	Paperwork
	9:00 – 10:00	Business plan
	10:00 – 12:00	Inspect
	1:00 – 5:00	Business plan
Thurs.	8:00 – 9:00	Paperwork
	9:00 – 11:00	Inspect
	12:00 – 3:00	Floor time/buyer tour
	3:00 – 6:00	Business plan
Fri.	8:00 – 8:45	Paperwork
	8:45 – 9:15	Office class
	9:30 – 12:00	Inspect
	1:00 – 5:00	Business plan
	7:00 – 8:00	Listing presentation
Sat.	9:00 – 12:00	Business plan
	1:00 – 4:00	Listing presentation/buyer tour
	4:00 – 5:00	Paperwork
Sun.	12:00 – 2:00	Business plan
	2:00 – 5:00	Open house or buyer tour
	5:00 – 6:00	Listing presentation

2. ***Business Support*** (activities that support the sales activities)
   - Previewing properties
   - Following up on transactions, making flyers, etc.
   - Sending out mailings (should not be considered a prime contact method)
   - Talking to loan officers and title companies
   - Attending meetings
   - Furthering education
   - Creating listing manuals

This list could be exhaustive. It's common for agents to "hide out" in support activities because they think they are not ready to talk to people. Watch out. This is a sign of creating the *wrong* activities in the business plan. These agents could end up becoming their own assistants—or someone else's!

Prioritized for You

This book is arranged to help you keep these activities in the right perspective. Each week, the business-producing activities are assigned first—the same way a successful agent plans a week. Figure 1.3 illustrates a prototype schedule that shows how much time you should be spending on each category. Use this schedule to check against the actual plan you design each week.

Principle Four: Prospect Like the Pros

One of the foundations of *Up and Running* is the *30 Days to Dollars* prospecting plan. This plan is built on the solid prospecting principles that make superstars successful. It uses the same target markets (sources of business) and numbers that superstars rely on to build a professional career. To create a high-number, highly profitable career, superstars:

- get at least 50 percent of their business from people they know (called referrals).
- gain business by promoting themselves on their successes.
- devise the particular prospecting program that meets their monetary and personality needs.
- get the majority of their business through proactive prospecting. (They find people—they don't wait for people to come to them.)

But you're not a superstar yet. *30 Days to Dollars* takes the superstars' business-development principles and translates them to your situation:

- *Work your best source of prospects.* At this point, you have no past customers. But you do have a great network of *people you know.* Start with them.

- *Promote success.* Next, superstars create more success by promoting their success. If you are a new agent, find someone in your office who will let you promote yourself on his or her success—a new listing taken, a sale, a listing sold, an open house. This method is called *circle prospecting.* (Refer to Section 7 and the audiotapes for an explanation of this process.)

- *Choose a prospecting method that matches your style.* Superstars create their own unique methods of prospecting based on their personality styles and relationships. You can, too. The *30 Days to Dollars* plan provides several methods for meeting prospects. (Refer to Section 7 and the audiotapes for more information on these methods.)

30 Days to Dollars translates these concepts that successful agents use to create ever-high-producing businesses to your situation, so that you can create the same kind of career base—quickly.

What about Cold Calling?

Cold calling means picking up the phone, dialing a stranger and asking for a lead. Although cold calling is the quickest way to get a lead, it isn't the most common way successful agents re-create their businesses. The *30 Days to Dollars* plan, which does not include cold calls, is modeled after the *best sources* of business. You start with the best source of prospects— people who already know you. Remember: *The warmer the relationship, the better chance you have of getting a lead.*

Your long-term goal is to create relationships that, over time, will deliver back referrals to you. Warm calling does a better job of creating those relationships.

What Works.   Too often agents want someone to give them a prospecting method that is guaranteed to work. However, what always works is: *The numbers.*

Cold calling does provide more contacts in the least amount of time. But it also brings more rejections and tougher contacts to convert. So, if you run out of people to talk to in the target markets recommended in *30 Days to Dollars,* go ahead and make cold calls—to anyone—using any method you want.

Figure 1.4   30 Days to Dollars

Each week you will have an assignment based on this plan.

Activity	Weekly Minimum
1. Contact people you know/meet.	
In-person calls	20
Phone calls	30
Follow-up mailers sent	50
2. Circle prospect in person.	**25**
3. Choose one additional activity from these.	
Farm Area in-person contacts	50
or	
FSBOs in-person or phone contacts	25
or	
Expired listings in-person or phone contacts	25
4. Hold public open houses.	1

Total weekly minimuim in-person/phone contacts: **100-125**

Figure 1.5 Your 30 Days to Dollars Plan (Prospecting)

Month: _____

Proactive Activities

	Week 1		Week 2		Week 3		Week 4		Totals	
	G	A	G	A	G	A	G	A	G	A
People you know/meet [50/week]										
Circle prospect [25/week]										
Farm [50/week]										
FSBOs [25/week]										
Expireds [25/week]										

Reactive Activities

	Week 1		Week 2		Week 3		Week 4		Totals	
	G	A	G	A	G	A	G	A	G	A
Open houses [1min]										

G=Goals
A=Actuals

Proactive means you go out and find a prospect.
Reactive means you wait for a prospect to come to you.

Figure 1.6   Monthly Activity Scorecard

Month: _____

Buyer Activities	Week 1		Week 2		Week 3		Week 4		Totals	
	G	A	G	A	G	A	G	A	G	A
Counseling Appointments w / buyers										
Qualified buyer showings										
# sales										

Listing Activities	Week 1		Week 2		Week 3		Week 4		Totals	
	G	A	G	A	G	A	G	A	G	A
Qualified listing appointments										
Marketable listings secured										
# of listings sold										

G=Goals   A=Actuals

A Script for Cold Calling.   A sales skill called *how to craft a sales call* is described in Section 7. Using this technique, you can craft a sales call to any target market. If you want to cold call in an area, just put together a script using this crafting technique. You will become a master cold caller because you not only have a script, you have the methodology behind the script.

If You Don't Know Anyone.   If you are new to your area, you will need to start with colder calls. However, before you begin cold calling, take another look at the people you come in contact with weekly. I'll bet you know more people than you think. Make a list of the service people you meet each week. Remember, every time you talk to someone, find out if they have a real estate need. Some of my best leads have been from my hairdresser!

Start Your Prospecting

30 Days to Dollars (see Figure 1.4) is a daily prospecting program that will *ensure a sale in your first 30 days* in the business. The activities are *prioritized for you*, so you can create the same kind of career that the superstars develop—from day one. Each week you will have an assignment based on this plan.

Figure 1.5 provides a different view of *30 Days to Dollars*. This grid allows you to set goals and keep track of your prospecting success. This is the first step in successful business implementation—setting short-term goals and measuring the results. Using this chart:

1. choose the markets you intend to work;
2. set goals for the number of people you intend to meet within these markets; and
3. log in your "actuals" (the number of contacts you actually make) each week.

The activities listed in Figure 1.5 will lead to results. These results are listed in the Monthly Activity Scorecard (see Figure 1.6). Think of these results as merely a continuation of the *sales cycle* that you started with the activities in *30 Days to Dollars*.

Step-by-Step to Dollars

It's important to note that this Monthly Activity Scorecard represents the sales process in order. Many business activity lists circulated in various new-agent classes do not reflect the natural progress of the sales cycle. Poorly organized scorecards misrepresent the sales process and how certain activities predict certain results. For example, you can't sell homes unless you show them to many buyers. You can't show and sell homes unless you first qualify the buyers. This scorecard is organized to help you plan effective sales activities.

How to use this scorecard:

1. Set goals for buyer and listing activities.
2. Use the numbers in Principle Five to compare your goals with proven ratios. You may want to adjust your goals.
3. Log in your "actuals."
4. Evaluate your progress.

Principle Five: Work the Numbers

Do you want to make a sale in your first month in the business? If so, you need to make at least *100* prospecting calls (in person or on the phone) each week, for the first four weeks you're in the business. This is your *ensurance plan.* The *30 Days to Dollars* plan has 100 calls per week built into the program. You will use and assess this program each week. With this method, you will learn an important *self-management tool*—the ability to measure and analyze your activities, and the results of those activities.

More Numbers: High Activities Reap Rewards

Remember the sales path? Let's add some numbers to that path, so we can project the results of our prospecting efforts.

On the sales side:

- *400* sales calls per month will return to you
- *12* qualifying appointments that will result in
- *8* showings that, if averaged over time, will result in *1* sale.

This means: If you want to sell one home per month, you need to talk to 400 people that month, find 12 people to qualify and show homes 8 times. You will, averaged over a few months, sell 1 home for every 8 times you put people in the car (not necessarily the same people—this is just a law of averages).

On the listing side:

- *400* contacts a month will result in
- *4* seller qualifying appointments that will lead to
- *2* qualified listings of which *1* listing will sell in market time.

The *Up and Running* plan has these numbers built into each week's business-producing activities. You will set a goal for *one sale* and *one listing* during the first four weeks of your business. In addition, you'll be setting standards for your business that will assure you of making a good living and building a solid career—from day one.

Up and Running Puts All the Business Principles Together

With these five principles, you have the basics of successful real estate business development. In addition, *Up and Running* provides an easy way of applying these principles to your situation. The following two tools will help you to shortcut your career challenges:

1. Weekly assignments and objectives to ensure that you reach your goals
2. A sample business-development plan, developed by agent Joan Smith

Joan Smith's Plan

To help clarify these business-development concepts, take a look at new agent Joan Smith's plan. Her complete business development plan, included in Section 10, shows how she planned her weekly, monthly and yearly goals to be successful quickly by using the principles and assignments in *Up and Running*.

Start with the Big Picture and Work to the Specifics.   Let's follow Joan as she creates her business development plan. First, using the grid on the next page, she sets her monetary goal. For Joan, that's $24,000 her first year in real estate ($2,000 higher than the median income for all REALTORS®—according to the latest National Association of REALTORS® survey). Because the average income per sale in her market is $2,000, she'll need to sell one home per month (or have one of her listings sell).

Know the Number of Activities Needed To Get a Result.   Joan's manager has told her that it takes approximately four listing appointments to list one home that sells in normal market time. It takes eight showing appointments to sell one home (This means eight groups of people in the car, not numbers of homes shown. They don't even have to be different groups. It's just the law of averages). Since Joan wants the result of one

Figure 1.7 Joan's Yearly Goals Translated to Monthly Goals and Activities

1. Set your monthly expectations

Your $ expectations this year

$$\$ 24,000 \div 12 = \$ 2,000$$

Monthly expectation in $

2. Translate $ to Units

Monthly expectation in $

Your $ earned sale per listing sold

Monthly unit goal

$$\$ 2,000 \div \$ 2,000 = \frac{1}{2} \quad \frac{1}{2}$$

Listing sold   Sales

3. Plan activities to meet unit goals

	Month 1	2	3	4	5	6
Listings Sold	0	0	1	0	1	0
Listings Taken	1	0	1	0	0	1
Listing Appts.	4	4	4	4	4	4
Sales	1	1	0	1	0	1
Showing Appts.	8	8	8	8	8	8
Contacts (From 30 Days to $)	400	300	200	200	200	200

Joan follows the same contact plan she used for her third month onward to schedule her contacts and business results for the remainder of the year. A planning page similar to this is available for you in Section 11.

Figure 1.8   Joan's Plan: From Breakeven to Profitability

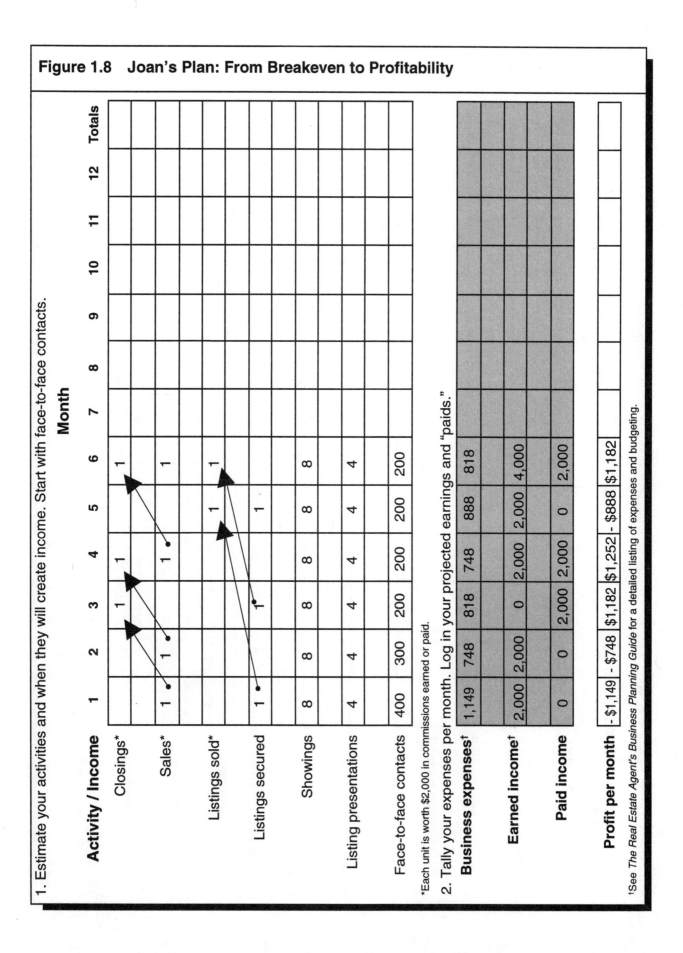

1. Estimate your activities and when they will create income. Start with face-to-face contacts.

Activity / Income	1	2	3	4	5	6	7	8	9	10	11	12	Totals
Closings*			1	1		1							
Sales*	1	1		1		1							
Listings sold*					1	1							
Listings secured	1		1		1								
Showings	8	8	8	8	8	8							
Listing presentations	4	4	4	4	4	4							
Face-to-face contacts	400	300	200	200	200	200							

*Each unit is worth $2,000 in commissions earned or paid.

2. Tally your expenses per month. Log in your projected earnings and "paids."

Business expenses†	1,149	748	818	748	888	818							
Earned income†	2,000	2,000	0	2,000	2,000	4,000							
Paid income	0	0	2,000	2,000	0	2,000							

Profit per month	- $1,149	- $748	$1,182	$1,252	- $888	$1,182							

†See *The Real Estate Agent's Business Planning Guide* for a detailed listing of expenses and budgeting.

Figure 1.9 From Breakeven to Profitability

1. Estimate your activities and when they will create income. Start with face-to-face contacts.

Month

Activity / Income	1	2	3	4	5	6	7	8	9	10	11	12	Totals
Closings													
Sales													
Listings sold													
Listings secured													
Showings													
Listing presentations													
Face-to-face contacts													

2. Tally your expenses per month. Log in your projected earnings and "paids."

Business expenses												
Earned income												
Paid income												

Profit per month

transaction per month, she knows she will have to put people in her car at least four times a month, and go to a listing presentation four times per month to ensure that she reaches her goal. Since she knows her fastest method of getting a check is through a sale, she sets a goal of eight showings per month. She also knows that her skill level isn't high at the beginning of her career, so she sets higher showing and listing presentation goals for herself than she will need to set later in her career.

Using *30 Days to Dollars* as an Activity Plan.   Note how Joan relates her monetary goals to her monthly and weekly activities (see Figure 1.7). The *30 Days to Dollars* plan suits Joan's needs. It gives her enough contacts to ensure that she reaches her goal—one sale or listing sold per month, which will result in her making her monetary goal of $24,000.

To schedule her contacts and business results for the remainder of the year, Joan follows the same contact plan she used for her third month onward. A similar planning page is illustrated in Section 11.

From Breakeven to Profitability

In order to plan your finances, you will need to complete the grid *From Breakeven to Profitability* (see Figures 1.8 and 1.9). This grid shows the relationship between business-cycle activities, time, expenses, income and breakeven point (the point where expenses equal income).

Joan's Breakeven Point.   The sample timeline in Figure 1.9 shows how Joan computed her breakeven and profit points. After reading Joan's timeline, complete the blank one in Figure 1.9 to provide you with the resources you need to successfully launch your career. The top part of the timeline allows you to fill in business-producing activities. Now, you can see *when* those activities will bring your desired results. The bottom part of the timeline allows you to write in your predicted *business expenses, income* from your sales results and *time* that you will receive this income. (For an in-depth itemization of start-up business expenses, refer to my book, *How about a Career in Real Estate?*)

Adapting Your Plan after the First Month.   After implementing the *30 Days to Dollars* plan for your first 30 days in the business, you will have enough leads to switch to a less aggressive (fewer initial sales calls) prioritized plan. Through tracking successful agents, I have found that agents that stay on the track described in *Up and Running* break even by month six.

All Your Self-Management Tools

You have just investigated the three tools needed for effective self-management:

1. *30 Days to Dollars*—provides a daily prospecting plan and measurement grids to track activities on the sales cycle

2. *Monetary Goals*—plans your one-year goals so you can backtrack to daily activities

3. *From Breakeven to Profitability*—demonstrates how daily activities lead to results; shows how expenses and income create a breakeven point; shows these variables through time (see Figure 1.8)

If your objectives are similar to Joan Smith's, simply use her prototype plans for each of the four areas. For reference, her entire plan is shown in Section 10. A set of blank planning pages for you is in Section 11.

Four Weeks to Becoming a Successful Agent

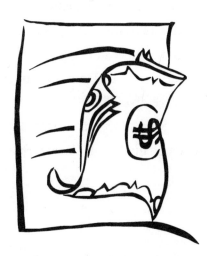

In the previous section, you learned the five principles of successful business management. However, these principles are only a part of what *Up and Running* will do for you. Sections 3 through 6 will provide specific business-producing assignments that will help you cover all the bases as you design your career. At the end of 30 days, you will have accomplished both business-development and business-support goals. Most importantly, you will have mastered the concepts of effective self-management in sales.

By fulfilling the activities to ***develop your business***, you will:

- have an effective new-agent business plan. You will have the tools to continue this planning process for long-term success.

- with the *30 Days to Dollars* plan, complete a minimum of:

    - 400 proactive prospecting calls

    - 8 qualified appointments to show

> - 1 sale
> - 4 listing appointments
> - 1 marketable listing

- know exactly how to start and continue the sales cycle.
- have invaluable experience in scheduling your own time to reap results. You will be on your way to effective time management.

By accomplishing the other assignments to *support your business*, you will:

- create a listing presentation manual.
- design a buyer qualifying/counseling manual.
- complete a listing form.
- carry out a market analysis.
- complete four purchase and sale agreements.
- learn the basics of financing and qualifying.
- observe your office's floor time.
- observe open houses.
- create a contact management system.
- practice the Seven Critical Sales Skills.

The How-To's

Many programs for new agents consist of numerous activities, but few programs show you exactly how to make sales calls. In *Up and Running*, I have included the "how" along with the "what." Sections 7 and 8 contain the critical sales communications skills needed to ensure your success. When you read the weekly assignments, you will see that the how-to's can be referenced from Sections 7 and 8. In addition, so that you can hear how these skills sound in sales communication, I have role-played them on audiotapes for each of the four weeks. Play these tapes again and again until these sales communications become natural to you.

Who Manages Your Program?

You do. You are in business for yourself, with your office and manager as support to you. This program is *driven* by you. If you want to capture the support of your manager, meet with him or her weekly. Go over your accomplishments in your business plan. In order to progress faster, get help in your support areas. Each weekly segment contains a checklist for accomplishments with a place for your manager's initials and comments. Use your manager's expertise; you'll get started better and faster.

As a manager, I have come to recognize common success traits in agents. One distinguishing quality is the ability to "demand" a manager's assistance. Inversely, agents who hang back, afraid to ask for the manager's guidance, will be less successful. I really appreciate new agents who consistently make appointments with me to let me know what they are doing, how they are doing it and how I can assist them. That's called *managing the manager*! Obviously, these new agents get lots of my attention, concern and positive strokes—the fuel for motivation.

Your goal is to understand and apply effective self-management techniques to create dynamic, professional long-term business success.

Who Will Manage Your Attitude?

Of course, after you learn the details and process needed to succeed in your plan, you must manage your own plan. The point of this book is to *teach you to manage your plan*, with your manager as "senior partner." Learning these planning concepts and completing these activities is relatively easy. They are, after all, simply a series of tasks. Now, let's add the *human being* to the process. Plans don't work—people do. As I speak to real estate companies across the United States, managers ask me if this plan works. I tell them: This plan does not work unless it's put to work *consistently* by qualified, dedicated real estate "careerists."

Sounds simple, doesn't it? Just do the work, and you'll be successful. Then why isn't everyone who enters real estate successful?

Behaviors versus Attitudes

Each year many people who enter the real estate field fail to earn the incomes they expected. (See *How about a Career in Real Estate?* for a study of new agents' short-term and long-term goals, contrasted with reality.) Many of these agents, disappointed with their incomes, leave the business within the first year. Some stay in the business, not earning what they expected, but subsidized by other incomes or spouses.

One reason for this contrast between goals and reality is: Often agents start the real estate business without a clear idea of their job description. They do not realize what new agents must do to be successful. They may think that showing up at the office five days a week to "take floor time"

Figure 2.1   A Successful Agent's Job Description

A successful agent consistently performs four categories of activities:

1. Business-developing plan

    • Find potential customers and clients by identifying target markets. Then, identify particular personal strengths. Create programs using strengths to reach these particular markets. Execute these programs daily.

    • Sample target markets

      – People you already know socially

      – People you know from former business

      – People you know from church/sports/organizations

      – People in your neighborhood/chosen neighborhood

      – People you meet in promoting seller's home

    Our agent's income and success is determined by the number of people contacted consistently in these target markets.

2. Sales activities generated as result of business-developing plan

    • Showing homes to qualified customers

    • Selling homes

    • Listing marketable properties to sell in normal market time

3. Activities that guarantee a check

    • Selling homes

    • Your listings sell

4. Preparation and support activities that supplement the business-producing activities

    • Preview properties

    • Paperwork/sales followup

    • Education

    • Meetings

By working an aggressive, personally tailored business plan, the successful agent ensures early income and long-term success.

guarantees a paycheck! They do not realize that their success depends on *frequently* starting and continuing the business cycle that is discussed in this book. (Also see *How about a Career in Real Estate?* for the "real scoop" about the business.) Then, after new agents have been in the business a few weeks, they discover that *their* job description does not bring the anticipated income. They find that a *successful* agent's job description is different from theirs (see Figure 2.1). Their enthusiasm about the business wanes. In effect, their *attitude* about the business has changed. I call these agents *no-start failures*. They did not have a chance to succeed in the business because they did not enter the business with an understanding of what was required to succeed. If agents do not understand the job, how can they commit to the work?

A tip for managers: Show *Up and Running* to your prospective agents during the interview process. Ask them to read the book and listen to the tapes, to project themselves performing these activities. Ask them if they will commit to doing this work—in the amount of time required and the numbers needed for success. Interviewees will appreciate your honest assessment of the behaviors and commitment levels required for success in today's real estate world. The net result will be that you'll hire winners.

How Our Attitudes Change with the Challenge

With *Up and Running*, you have a clear idea of what successful agents do to launch a career. You have committed to this plan—this job description. End of discussion, right? Wrong. All of us have our "ups and downs" as we struggle through anything new. Change is difficult.

As a new agent, you start the business with:

* enthusiasm,
* confidence,
* high self-esteem, and
* excitement.

You tell your manager that you're tenacious, that you can handle rejection. The manager need not worry that you'll do the activities because you're a self-starter and can motivate yourself. Then you start performing the activities. You've always thought of yourself as a good communicator. However, as you prospect, you find it difficult to communicate. People somehow create many ways to reject you. You've always liked people, and you sense they like you. Yet they act differently with you now that you're in *sales*. People make up stories to avoid you, say they "have a friend in the business," get information from you but do not give you information, promise to meet with you at the office—and don't show up. You experience feelings of:

- rejection,
- frustration,
- impatience,
- self-doubt, and
- inadequacy.

Your image of yourself is tested. Which is the real *you*? The one who feels confident, tenacious and a self-starter? Or the one who feels rejected, frustrated, inadequate and full of self-doubt? Your attitude about the business—and yourself—is in danger of shifting from *positive* to *negative*.

Attitudes Can Change in Seconds

Each day, hour and minute, you evaluate your feelings about the business. Your *experiences* as you perform the activities in this plan fuel this evaluation. Your *conclusions* are based on your personal belief system. It's not the activities that cause you to have a certain attitude about the business, but the conclusions you draw from your experiences with these activities. Let's say you have knocked on 50 doors without getting a lead. What do you conclude? Agents who will fail conclude that "this won't work in this area." Agents who will succeed imagine themselves one step closer to a lead with every rejection. These agents realize that they must experience many rejections to get success.

Managing Attitude Shifts

Managers can teach new agents what activities to do, how to do them and how to monitor them to evaluate effectiveness. Using the forms provided in this book, managers and agents can track agents' actual *behaviors* each day. But who will keep track of changing attitudes? Who will manage the conclusions about these activities? These emotional evaluations flit through a new agent's head hundreds of times a day. *How* these constantly changing attitudes are managed determines whether or not the agent will succeed.

What Agents Want

According to a recent survey of real estate salespeople, one of the most important services agents want from their manager is to *provide positive motivation.* Sounds easy, doesn't it? Part of it is. It's not difficult to create a positive atmosphere in the office. It is difficult to find out what motivates each individual (everyone has different motivators). And it is more difficult to design a motivational program to fit each agent's need—time in the business, motivators, outside influences, etc. However, it's *very* difficult for a manager to manage the constant flux of attitudes, to catch agents when they are falling into depression and to pump them up. Why? First, agents' attitudes change hundreds of times a day. When agents get down, they usually talk to themselves—negatively. How can managers manage agents' ups and downs? They can't. But they can *teach* new agents how to manage their ups and downs.

Becoming a Managing Master of Your Attitudes

Managing your attitude requires three steps:

1. *Recognize your attitude will change* about the business as you do the activities in the business.
2. *Acknowledge* each time you draw a conclusion about your activities.
3. *Develop a process* for controlling your conclusions.

Evaluating Your Attitudinal Process

To evaluate and manage your attitude, try this simple, effective method. In a notebook, divide each page into six columns:

- Self-talk
- Conclusions of your self-talk
- Positive attitude
- Negative attitude
- Revised conclusion/revised attitude
- Belief

As you go about your business day, keep the notebook handy. Write down each time you talk to yourself—positively and negatively. Let's say you just held an open house. As you are leaving, you say to yourself: "What's wrong with me? I thought I was a good communicator, but these people coming into my open house won't tell me anything." Write down the conclusion you drew: *Maybe I'm not cut out for this business.* Note these thoughts in the proper column—*positive* or *negative*. Obviously, the above comment and conclusion would go in the negative column.

Managing Your Conclusions for a Positive Attitude

Studies show that most self-talk is *negative,* which naturally leads to a *negative* conclusion. People will talk to themselves about this conclusion 10 to 20 times and convince themselves that this conclusion is true! Thus, when agents conclude that they cannot be successful in open houses, that idea plays again and again in their minds until they change their positive attitude about their success in the business—and form a new belief about their ability to communicate.

You can stop this insidious, although natural, process by replacing it with a new process. To do this, you must replace your natural inclination of *negative* self-talk, repeated again and again, with some *positive* self-talk, repeated again and again.

Retraining Your Mind

Is this the conclusion about open houses that you really want to draw? Is this the attitude that will ensure your success in this business? Can you change your conclusion and attitude? Tough-minded, success-oriented people can adjust their conclusions and attitudes about their experiences to reach their goals. They experience the same rejection, self-doubt, frustration and anxieties that failure-oriented people do. The only difference is that these tough-minded people have developed a mental system to reinterpret their conclusions. It's as simple as substituting a different conclusion, along with a change in attitude. So, go back to your notebook, and write a new conclusion to your experience. For the example above, it might be: *Based on my results, I'm not as good a communicator as I thought I was. I need to improve my communication skills. I can get these skills by taking the Dale Carnegie Sales Skill Course, by observing agents who are successful at open houses and by practicing my new skills."*

Making Your New Conclusion Believable

The last column in your notebook, belief, is very important. If you don't *believe* that you can create a new conclusion, you will not take the action steps. In the *belief* column, add a statement that backs up your opinion about skills enhancement. It might be: *I know that, if other agents can be successful getting appointments at open houses, I can be, too. It's just a matter of my learning, practicing and perfecting the skills required."*

Being Tough-Minded Enough to Succeed

The ability to *consciously* control your attitude is a skill that can be learned. To ensure your success in real estate, assume that you need to develop tough-mindedness. By following the steps outlined, you can become tough-minded enough to succeed in real estate.

Many excellent self-help books on how to create a positive mental attitude, as well as courses and videos on self-esteem, exist. One of the best courses, a successful process developed by Lou Tice, is offered at his Pacific Institute, Seattle, Washington.

Controlling your attitude is simple if you recognize that it's a *skill* that can be learned. It takes practice, tenacity and patience. But isn't it worth it if it ensures your success in real estate? You have a proven, successful, activity-based, business-developing program in *Up and Running.* You have a manager committed to your success. You have the tools to retrain your mind and control your attitude. You are set for success!

The Manager's Role

It's tough out there. Agents enter the real estate business with enthusiasm, hope and determination. Then they find out what rejection means, and their enthusiasm quickly withers under the stress of starting anew.

Managers can help. This book offers new agents (and those attempting to re-jump-start their careers) a program that will ensure a successful career. However, to start and continue a challenging program (whether it's a diet or a new job), every agent needs *encouragement*—not just "atta boy, keep going" kind of support but *real, specific, constructive guidance and feedback* that will help the agent to build a successful daily plan and to know that it is working.

How Managers Can Help Agents and Still Have Time To Run the Office

In their quest to make a profit, managers must do everything from counsel agents to run the administrative part of the office. It's difficult for managers to provide new agents the guidance needed to get their careers off to a quick, successful start. This program relieves managers' concerns because it provides the plan and resources new agents need to begin a successful career.

This program is based on the assumption that new agents are truly in business for themselves—with their managers as *consultants.* Agents are responsible for completing each weekly assignment. Managers meet with the agent weekly (the agent sets the appointment) to review the agent's accomplishments and to add information specific to the office and market area. The grids entitled Accomplishments in Sections 3 through 6 provide managers and agents an opportunity to review the areas completed each week.

Each of us, as managers, is committed to the success of each new agent we hire. *Up and Running* gives managers the foundation to build a business relationship that agents will appreciate throughout their entire careers.

Manager–Agent "Success" Agreement

As in any successful partnership, the new agent has the best chance to succeed when the agent and manager work closely together. To ensure that manager and agent are sharing mutual expectations, use the Agreement To Ensure That You're *Up and Running* (see Figure 2.2).

> *Note to managers: With all the tasks we have to achieve, providing the time and support necessary to ensure a new agent's fast start is difficult. For the past ten years, I have developed another support system to work in tandem with* Up and Running. *It's called* "Crosscoaching": A Proven Mentor Program. *(See References for details.)*

An Overview of Your Four Weeks

Each week, for four weeks, you will complete the following activities:

1. *Create your weekly and daily plan.* Use the provided planners; refer back to the Prototype Schedule and *30 Days to Dollars* plan. Be sure to keep a balance of business-producing activities and support activities. Ask your manager to assess the balance of your plan. Creating your plan and assessing it, two of the most valuable self-management tools in *Up and Running,* provide the basis for making good business judgments throughout your entire career.

2. *Use the* **30 Days to Dollars** *plan and grid.* The business activity plan is provided to you each week, so you can easily plan your activities and track results.

3. *Track business-producing activities.* For each day and for the week, a grid is provided to help you track your results. This way, you will create your own *ratios of success*, so that you can analyze and make adjustments to your business in the future.

4. *Practice and apply new sales skills.* To optimize your contact with potential buyers and sellers, *Up and Running* provides the critical sales skills you need to save time and to convert more prospects to real buyers and sellers.

Figure 2.2   Agreement To Ensure That You're *Up and Running*

I, _____, agree to complete all the assignments in *Up and Running in 30 Days* because I intend to design a career to be successful quickly and professionally.

I want support from my manager, so I agree to make an appointment with my manager weekly. During that appointment, I will review my work for that week and my plan for the next week.

I understand that doing the work according to the priorities and numbers in *Up and Running in 30 Days* is the professional's method of beginning my business.

To ensure that I get the most from my work, I expect my manager to:

• meet with me weekly for at least one-half hour;

• help me keep my activities prioritized correctly;

• provide assistance in my development of specific business methods;

• provide me any resources necessary to complete the assignments; and

• provide the support and encouragement necessary to begin a successful career.

I understand it's my business, and I agree to manage it according to the principles in *Up and Running in 30 Days* because I want to create a successful, high-producing, professional career.

_____   _____
                Agent   Manager

Date of this agreement: _____ End of program: _____

5. *Complete business support activities.* You need confidence in your ability to make sales calls. These business-supporting activities provide the confidence you need to create a top-producing business.

6. *Meet with your manager for support, information and encouragement.* It's difficult to "go it alone," and your manager is committed to your success. *Up and Running* provides a solid foundation for communication between you and your manager.

Turning Contacts into *Real* Buyers and Sellers

Besides the business-managing and weekly assignments in *Up and Running,* there are two other critical parts to this system to ensure that you get results from your sales efforts:

1. The Seven Critical Sales Skills
2. Qualifying buyers and sellers

Seven Critical Sales Skills

In this four-week plan, you will develop valuable sales skills. A foundation of *Up and Running,* these sales skills are introduced and explained in Section 8 and on the audiotapes. Each week you will practice and apply new skills, developing them in five ways:

- Listening to the audiotapes
- Reading the synopsis of the prospecting methods/scripts in the appendix
- Interviewing agents
- Practicing these skills with a fellow professional
- Practicing these skills in the field

Your sales skills form the basis to begin your sales career. Use them, adapt them, apply them to all situations that require effective communication skills.

Sales Skills—"Specialty" Communication

Do you consider yourself a good communicator? Most people who enter real estate feel one of their biggest strengths is their ability to communicate. When I mention communicate, what do you think of? To many of us, to communicate means *to talk*. If we're good talkers, we assume we would be good salespeople. When we enter real estate, we take courses in finance, escrow, title insurance and building inspections in order to *talk to strangers (potential customers and clients) with authority.* After all, if anyone asked us a question, we would be embarrassed if we didn't know the answer. And we start talking our way right out of a real estate career!

Why? Because people don't care how much you *know* until they know how much you *care.* How do you show that you care about others? Ask them questions; listen to them. People want to be *listened to, understood and empathized with.* Instead of learning facts and figures to dazzle prospects, the most important communication skill to hone is *listening.*

To become a good listener, practice the following skills that effective listeners have developed:

- Listen for inflections, pauses, the pace—the "music" of the talk rather than the "words."
- Actively acknowledge the talker (e.g., yes, okay, hmmm).
- Repeat what the talker said to be sure you correctly understood it.
- Ask for more clarification of what the listener said.
- Avoid jumping to conclusions and talking.

Are You a Good Listener?

Generally, people assume that they're good listeners. But, in truth, most people just listen carefully enough to get the gist and long enough to get ready to talk! They're thinking about what they're going to say rather than listening effectively. Recently, I was teaching a large group of managers how to apply counseling techniques for use with their agents. One principle of counseling is that, to solve the problem, we must get to the *root* of the problem. Often the agent's problem isn't really a problem but a symptom. In the class, I showed managers a proven counseling process that worked. Then I asked the managers to use this process, which required them to demonstrate all the listening skills in the class. Although they resisted taking the time to probe, listen and clarify, the managers acknowledged that the process worked. Following the process, they restrained from offering a pat solution and, as they probed further, discovered that the problem was different from what they had first assumed. Their initial solution, had they offered it, would have been wrong.

The same holds true for you with your customers and clients. They have problems, objections, beliefs. You must take the time to find out exactly what is on your customers' minds and in their hearts to help them meet their needs. *Effective listening is the most important communication skill to develop for a successful real estate career.*

What Do Sales Skills Have To Do with Listening?

I hope that I have convinced you that listening is the most important communication skill to develop for success in sales. But how can you listen if people won't talk to you? You hold an open house, but people avoid you. You get a call on an ad, but the caller doesn't offer any information. How do you "prime the pump"—get people to talk to you—so that you can listen?

Learn To Ask Questions—The Right Questions.   When I was a child, my aunts would chide my mother because she always took the time to answer my questions—my *hundreds* of questions! My aunts thought my mother gave me too much detail, too much attention, too much time. But I learned so much because my mother treated my questions with respect. I learned that you learn by asking questions, not by talking. I learned that, when I got my mom to talk, she forgot to ask *me* any questions—like, had I practiced the piano that day. As long as I kept her talking, I controlled the conversation!

Control the Conversation.   Let's go back to the open house scenario. The prospects come in. Their objective is to get information from you while keeping secret any information about themselves. They know the principle of controlling conversations. Being effective communicators, they ask, "What's the price of this home?" Ready to prove that you are a knowledgeable real estate agent, you relate the price, the terms, the insulation value, the prices in the neighborhood and your opinion about world politics in general (just kidding!). You're really communicating—you think. The prospects thank you and walk out. You kick yourself. You didn't get an appointment.

What went wrong? You proved that you were knowledgeable. Why didn't the prospects volunteer information—give you their names, social security numbers and undying loyalty? Because you didn't *ask*. They got the information they wanted and controlled the conversation; you got nothing. This is not effective communication. Yet I have observed this scenario dozens of times. With effective listening and questioning skills, you could remedy this situation.

Listening and questioning skills are right here—in a sales format. The Seven Critical Sales Skills (see Section 8) are designed to put you in control—to help you ask the right questions and really listen to your potential customers and clients. These are simply effective communication skills adapted to a sales format.

Refining Your Communication Skills

Few agents, including experienced salespeople and managers, are as skilled at listening and questioning as they could be. To refine your communication abilities, practice listening and questioning skills until you:

- *really* understand customers' and clients' needs;
- can define *exactly* what the customer means when he says he wants a *deal* (each customer has a different definition);
- are *listening* two-thirds of the time you're with a customer, and *talking* one-third of the time;
- get at least one solid appointment per open house;
- get most of the people at your open house to share their real estate needs with you;
- get the names and phone numbers, along with appointments, if they qualify, of three-quarters of the people who call you during your floor time;
- can discover the dominant buying motive (motivation) of each buyer and seller you work with—in your first interview; and
- can consistently remove barriers and communicate effectively with buyers and sellers to get them the homes they want—and want to sell.

Qualifying Buyers and Sellers

According to new agents, the most difficult challenge to master is time management. Much of these problems come from an inability to control buyers and sellers. To get you off on the right foot and to help you spend your time effectively, use the following four sales resources to qualify your buyers and sellers.

For buyers:

1. Qualified buyer checklist
2. Buyer log

For sellers:

3. Seller log
4. Marketable listing checklist

As you qualify buyers and sellers each week, log them in on the grids (see Section 9). Be sure the buyers and sellers meet the standards you set.

Before you set a buyer or seller appointment, ask yourself if the buyer or seller meets the standards set on these grids. After the appointment, go back to the grid and requalify your prospect. Instead of working with poorly qualified buyers and sellers (as many new agents do), simply go back into the field and find more prospects. Take the attitude that your prospect is *lucky* to be working with you!

Developing Your Qualifying Skills

Listening, Questioning, Qualifying. To review the value of communication skills, listening makes the difference in an agent's career success. However, an agent can't listen to buyers or sellers if they don't talk. To encourage customers and clients to talk, the most effective method is to ask questions. Although this pattern of asking questions to get the other person to talk may seem obvious, it is not our normal social pattern.

Evaluating Social Conversations. Tomorrow, listen to three social conversations. How do the people proceed? How many questions does each person ask of the other? How many follow-up questions are asked? Does the person asking the question get impatient and want to talk? Does this person look anxious to give an answer? This is normal social habit: Communication means making statements and expecting the other person to listen.

Sales Communication Is Different. In sales, this social exchange method of communication just doesn't work when you need information from the prospect to start and continue the sales cycle. To discover the prospect's reasons for purchasing, desires or motivations, you must consistently ask questions and listen. You must talk one-third of the time and listen two-thirds. What a difference! It takes time to change social communication habits to sales communication habits. However, agents who *never* learn to change their patterns are not very successful.

How To Develop Qualifying Questions

The grids in *Up and Running* for qualifying buyers and sellers (see Section 9) are used by successful, experienced agents. Use these grids to develop qualifying questions to use in the interview process for buyers and sellers. First, let's look at the grids for sellers.

Qualifying Sellers: A Priority

Following is a common scenario for new agents (even some experienced agents still fall into this trap): A prospective client calls during your floor time and requests a market analysis on his home. You're so excited that you make an appointment without asking any qualifying questions. You inspect the home and do all the work required to complete a market analysis. You return to the home and give the prospective client your complete, full-color, 20-page market analysis. You don't hear from him. You call and find out that he wanted the market analysis to give to his niece, who just entered the real estate field, for an assignment in her training school. You feel used. However, the prospective client feels that, since you provided the market analysis service without qualifying him, he got what he wanted. And he assumes that you got what you wanted. *Was* it what you wanted?

Setting Qualifying Standards for Your Level of Professionalism

To avoid feeling used, act like a pro. Take doctors, for example. When you go into a doctor's office for the first time, what happens? You fill out a form (the doctor is qualifying you). If you don't answer questions on the form, the nurse gives the form back to get the answers to those questions— or you don't get to see the doctor!

Qualifying the Seller at the Beginning of the Process

Generally, to list a property, agents use a two-step process:

1. *Qualify* the seller and the property for salability.
2. *Present* your marketing plan, including pricing, to the seller.

Qualifying starts in the first phone conversation with the seller. The agent needs to find out:

- what the seller wants, and
- why the seller wants it.

Looking at the grid (see Figure 2.3), what questions would you need to ask over the phone to decide whether you want to visit a prospective client's home? Jot down these questions. Then, query three top agents in your office about the questions they ask—and the answers they look for—before they

Figure 2.3   For Sellers: Qualified Listing Appointments

Date of Presentation	Name	Address	Want To Sell	Both Home	2 Hours Pre-Scheduled	How Much $ Want	Marketing Presentation Completed	Results

will make an appointment to begin the listing process. For example, if you ask the seller why he or she wants a market analysis and the reply is, "For insurance purposes," what would you do?

Qualifying continues when the agent visits the seller and inspects the property. During the first appointment, the agent's goal is to ascertain whether he wants to list the property.

Think of it this way. It's much like the doctor who asks qualifying questions rather than jumps to conclusions. Why? Jumping to conclusions could mean a wrong diagnosis—and a wrong treatment. To be successful in real estate, agents should take the same approach. Ask sellers lots of questions about themselves. Why? You are qualifying them. What are some things you would want to know about a seller *before* committing to do a marketing plan? In other words, what are some *qualifying* questions? For example, two important questions are: When do you want to move? Where are you moving?

After you've outlined some qualifying questions, query three listing agents in your office about the questions they ask sellers to qualify them prior to "diagnosing treatment"—creating a marketing plan.

Gathering Information.   Many agents think that their job during the first visit is to gather information about the home. They do not realize that it's more important to their career to qualify the seller than it is to inspect the home! So, they focus on the number of bathrooms and bedrooms and forget that the seller's motivation, loyalty and needs must be understood and met. This is the information that forms the basis for your marketing plan.

Establishing Professional Boundaries.   You have qualified the seller over the phone, inspected the property and asked the seller numerous questions. Next, you complete the research on the property and prepare the marketing plan (including the pricing analysis). Now, you're ready to present your marketing plan to the seller.

Pause a minute. Before you make the second appointment with the seller, consider what would cause you *not* to make that second appointment. What professional boundaries have you established to ensure that you do not waste your time with unmotivated sellers and unmarketable properties?

What Happens When Agents Have Established Boundaries?   Let's look at an agent who's made a tough, professional personal boundary of not listing properties that she has determined will not sell in normal market time. This agent will not list properties that are more than three percent over her analysis of what that property will actually sell for. Why this personal boundary? This "pro" wants to establish a name for herself as a REALTOR®

who only lists properties that sell. Her reputation depends on "sold" signs on properties. Obviously, this reputation will attract only serious sellers, who appreciate her professional attitude. During the first appointment, if she determines that the sellers want more money for their home than her initial professional opinion indicates, she will not make the next appointment. Why should she waste her time and ruin her reputation? Or, if, after the second appointment, the sellers wants more money for their home than her expert opinion warrants, she won't list the home.

Recently, I saw how this strategy works. An agent in my office prepared a marketing plan for a seller. However, since the competition priced the property $50,000 higher than our agent, the seller chose to list with the competition. Unfortunately, the competition did not work in our area and used the wrong homes to diagnose the home's selling challenges.

The seller, initially, was pleased with the listing agent because he listed the home at such a high price. Of course, the seller expected selling agents to bring customers. However, agents who wanted to create trust and loyalty with their buyers would not show the overpriced home to their buyers. So the seller saw few potential buyers.

After three months of lost marketing time, the disillusioned seller listed with our agent at the right price. However, irreparable damage had been done to all parties involved. National surveys show that this added time on market will cost the seller thousands of dollars. Homes that are on the market a long time sell for less than if they were listed at the right price and sold quickly. (Remember Charles Revson's marketing truism: *Create demand.* When buyers compete, the price goes up.) Because the first listing agent did not create a satisfied customer, he or she will not get any return business. Unfortunately, the agent who lists the home the second time around won't have as satisfied a customer as if he had been able to list the home first—at the right price. In conclusion, overpricing properties brings negative results to sellers, listing agents and selling agents.

Now, let's look at how the second seller grid (see Figure 2.4 Evaluate Property Salability) can help you establish qualifying questions and professional boundaries.

Evaluate Property Salability

Sellers qualify agents. And good agents carefully qualify sellers. How confident would you feel if your doctor did not ask you any questions but simply prescribed aspirin every time you came to the office?

Sellers' confidence in an agent is raised when they know that the agent has established certain criteria for marketing property. Why waste sellers' time—and money—if the property won't sell? Look at the salability

Figure 2.4   Evaluate Property Salability

1. Property listed at competitive price.   Yes____   No____

2. Full-term listing agreement.   Yes____   No____

3. Seller to complete obvious repairs/cleaning prior to showing.   Yes____   No____

4. Easy access (e.g., key, phone for showing).   Yes____   No____

5. Yard sign.   Yes____   No____

6. Immediate possession.   Yes____   No____

7. Extras included (e.g., appliances).   Yes____   No____

8. Available for first tour.   Yes____   No____

9. Government terms available.   Yes____   No____

10. Owner financing available.   Yes____   No____

11. Below market down payment.   Yes____   No____

12. Below market interest rate.   Yes____   No____

13. Post-dated price reduction.   Yes____   No____

14. Market commission.   Yes____   No____

15. In my evaluation, this property will sell within listed market range, in normal market time for this area.   Yes____   No____

16. My credibility as a professional will be enhanced by listing this property.   Yes____   No____

checklist in Figure 2.4. What questions for the first and second visits would provide information to help you decide whether or not to list this property? What questions and criteria would you add for your own professional boundaries? How could you use this list with sellers?

What's your bottom line objective with sellers? Is it to list property? To post signs? To sell as many of your listings as possible? To list only properties that will sell in normal market time? To create high levels of customer satisfaction to get lots of referral business? To create an image for yourself as a real estate agent whose properties always sell quickly? Establish your boundaries based on your desired levels of professionalism. You decide. It's your career.

Qualifying Buyers: A New Approach

With the changes in agency representation, you will consider working with buyers exactly as you have always worked with sellers. Qualify and list buyers to work with you throughout the entire process of purchasing a home. This means that, when you first meet a buyer, begin the qualifying process. For example, as you are holding open house, you meet a potential buyer. Some questions you need to ask are:

- How long have you been looking for a home?
- When do you want/need to move?
- Have you been prequalified by a lender?

What questions would you ask before you decide to make an appointment to show the buyer homes? What are your professional boundaries? Would you show a buyer homes *without* knowing the answers to several key questions? To discover other key questions, ask three agents in your office what preliminary qualifying questions help them to qualify a buyer. Ask them their professional boundaries.

The Qualifying or Consulting Session. To avoid making a poor buying decision, today's buyers need a lot of information *before* they look at homes. Buyers need a way to get this information from someone they can trust. Here's where you come in. Develop a method to meet with and consult with potential buyers *before* they begin looking at properties. Develop informational materials. At the same time, wrap into this informational system a qualifying questionnaire. You will not only provide information to buyers, you will qualify them in a professional manner. You are choosing the buyer as the buyer is selecting you.

Figure 2.5   Qualified Buyers

Log a record of your appointments throughout the program.

Date of Qualify Meeting	Name	Address	Qualify Checklist Used	Both @ Qualifying Session	# Showings	Sales

A System To Assist You. Because listing buyers is a new concept, I have developed a system for you to use to inform and qualify buyers. This system/method, similar to the listing systems for sellers you use through your company, is called *List the Buyer System* and consists of a 24-page booklet for buyers, which explains the purchasing process and your value in this process. A 2-page questionnaire with the critical questions you need to ask buyers is included. Most questionnaires for buyers focus on their physical needs in a home (e.g., number of bedrooms, baths). Unfortunately, the buyers' real needs, their emotional needs, are not addressed. The questionnaire developed in *List the Buyer* assists the buyer and agent in pinpointing the root of the concern, so that the agent can pick the right homes to show the buyer. In addition to the booklet for buyers, there is a confidential separate section for agents on how to create added value and credibility, and how to earn respect for your services. There's also information on how to create loyalty during the sale—and after. The agents' main concerns when working with buyers are to create value-added services that set them apart from the average "licensee"—so the buyer will have reasons to choose them exclusively.

The Grids for Qualifying Buyers

Now, let's look at how the following grids can assist you as you develop qualifying questions and professional boundaries for working with buyers.

The first grid (see Figure 2.5) helps you to keep track of your appointments. Note the "both at qualifying session" column. We have learned that showing homes to only one person when two are buying is an exercise in futility. You need to get to know both parties, for their motivations may be entirely different from one another. I recommend that you draw a professional boundary at showing homes to one party over a period of time without the other.

Note the "number of showings" column in Figure 2.5. (This is important data to keep.) The rule of thumb says that you must put people (not the same people) in your car eight times to sell a home. Let's say your goal is to sell one home per month. How many times per week, on average, must you put people in your car? Right. Twice. However, since you're new at this game, your conversion ratios may be different. Keep track, and, if necessary, adjust your numbers to reach your goals.

What the Conversion Ratios Will Tell You. Considering that the agent's greatest concern is time management, think of the time wasted if agents put people in their cars and showed them homes without qualifying them! Yet, agents frequently do this. Janis, an experienced agent, had shown homes 25 times in the last few weeks, yet had made no sales. She

Figure 2.6 Evaluate Your Customer's Potential

Rate on a scale of 1–4 (4 being the highest)

1. Customer is motivated to purchase.
   (Rate each spouse/partner separately.)   1   2   3   4

2. Customer is realistic about price range expectations.   1   2   3   4

3. Customer is open and cooperative.   1   2   3   4

4. Customer will purchase in a timely manner.   1   2   3   4

5. Customer is a referral source and will provide referrals.   1   2   3   4

6. Customer has agreed that you will be his or her
   exclusive agent.   1   2   3   4

7. Agent has established a positive rapport with
   customer.   1   2   3   4

8. Customer will meet with loan officer.   1   2   3   4

9. Customer answered financial questions openly.   1   2   3   4

10. Customer has no other agent obligations.   1   2   3   4

11. If customer has home to sell, he or she is realistic
    about price.   1   2   3   4

12. Customer will devote sufficient time to purchasing
    process.   1   2   3   4

13. Both spouses/partners will be available to look for home.   1   2   3   4

Is this customer worthy of your time, energy and expertise?

was frustrated because she had been working so hard with no results. What was wrong? Perhaps she wasn't qualifying buyers or showing the wrong homes. If she had used a good qualifying questionnaire and learned to ask questions and to listen, she would have shown the right homes. Perhaps she wasn't closing. Again, if Janis had used a good qualifying questionnaire, she would have known the buyers' motivation—and could have helped the buyers make a buying decision at the right time. Successful results depend on a well-crafted, well-practiced, well-organized consulting/qualifying meeting.

As you read the criteria for evaluating your customer's potential (see Figure 2.6), qualifying questions will become obvious. Jot these questions down. Ask three agents in your office about their qualifying questions. Ask about their professional boundaries. What will yours be? When I was a new agent, no one told me to qualify buyers. I just put everyone who wanted to look at homes in my car. I saw lots of homes, but I sure got tired! Finally, I developed a qualifying process. Guess what? Buyers respected me, they complied with my requests and they met my standards. Why? Because I had created something of value—something other agents did not provide. In my *List the Buyer System* (see References), I have listed dozens of services that I provided to loyal buyers—and you can provide—to build value.

Establishing a Value-Added Service Approach

Studies show that buyers think that the greatest service REALTORS® provide is showing listed homes! If that were true, they could choose any agent. But you and I know that the services agents provide are wide and varied. Some agents don't even call prospects back! Some agents have other jobs and work only part-time in the profession. Other agents don't update their knowledge and skills, so they can't help buyers with new information. The list goes on and on.

To create buyer loyalty, establish your own list of value-added services. Where will your level of professionalism be? After establishing your list, decide how to communicate these services to buyers early in the building-rapport stage. With your professional stance and your ability to communicate, you have started the listing-the-buyer process, which will be a win-win for both buyer and agent.

When does a new agent get tough about qualifying? You're probably thinking: If I qualify sellers and buyers as Carla suggests, I won't have nearly as many listings as lots of agents I know. I won't be putting as many people in my car. I'm not sure I'm ready to be tough—yet. Okay. *When* and *how* will you get tougher?

Many agents think that they will "get tough later." Bob, an agent in my office, refused to qualify buyers. He simply tried to talk to them between showing homes, while driving them around. He said that he would qualify them better when he was more successful. Bob lasted in the business only a few months. He felt people took advantage of him; he had trouble closing; he thought that closing techniques would solve his buyer problems. In truth, though, closing techniques are inconsequential when compared to a great qualifying system. In today's world of sophisticated buyers, qualifying systems with prioritized information are the key to sales success.

More Prospecting Solves the "Tough" Dilemma.   Don't do what I did—wasting your time hauling unqualified non-prospects around is not fun or productive. Start right—prospect for hundreds of potentially qualified prospects. Be tough when you qualify them. You will be able to list only qualified properties because you will have too many potential listings to spend time with uncooperative sellers and overpriced listings.

Managers are not impressed with busy work; they are impressed with *results*. A listing isn't a result; a *sold* listing is a result. Be kind to yourself. Start the business with a careerist approach. Develop professional standards and boundaries. Treat yourself with respect, and buyers and sellers will respect you. Using the four qualifying grids automatically boosts your professionalism. Here's to great qualifying!

Week One

You are now familiar with the concepts of successful business development. You have some insights about managing your attitude. You understand the numbers involved in planning your business. You are ready to translate all this knowledge into action. In Sections 3 through 6, I have provided a detailed, precise weekly action plan to ensure your success. In each week's plan, you'll first see the objectives—your short-term goals for the week. To keep your priorities correct, these objectives are divided between business development and business support. In each group, your weekly activities are outlined. Along with accomplishing your sales goals, you will be gaining sales skills. At the end of each week, you will tally your accomplishments to share with your manager. Dive in now—start creating your picture of success!

Objectives

Business Development

- Begin *30 Days to Dollars* with the best sources of prospects—people you know.
- Make 100 sales calls.
- Get two qualified buyer leads.
- Get two qualified seller leads.
- Show homes to two qualified buyer groups.
- Go to at least one listing appointment.
- Apply three new sales skills in sales situations.

Business Support

- Create a workable weekly plan based on good business principles. Translate this plan to a daily plan.

- Become comfortable with office operations.

- Get a working knowledge of the listing agreement and the information sources for that agreement.

- Get a working knowledge of market analysis and the information sources for that analysis. Learn how to package a market analysis. Learn three methods of countering sellers' objections to pricing.

- Practice three new sales skills.

Preparation for Reactive Activities

- Understand how public open houses draw potential customers and clients.
- Get a working knowledge of the floor time system in your office (if you have floor time available).

After this week, reactive activities won't be discussed. See your office training program for specific training in open houses and floor time.

Figure 3.1   Your Weekly Plan

Week: _____

Name: _____

Time	Monday	Tuesday	Wednesday	Thursday	Friday	Saturday	Sunday
7–8							
8–9							
9–10							
10–11							
11–12							
12–1							
1–2							
2–3							
3–4							
4–5							
5–6							
6–7							
7–8							
8–9							

Figure 3.2   Daily Planner

Date:_____

Priorities: Accomplished   Notes:

1._____   ☐   _____

2._____   ☐   _____

3._____   ☐   _____

4._____   ☐   _____

5._____   ☐   _____

6._____   ☐   _____

7._____   ☐   _____

8._____   ☐   _____

9._____   ☐   _____

10._____   ☐   _____

	Contacts	Qualified Leads	Listing Appointments	Showings
Activity				

	Listings Obtained	Sales	Listings Sold
Results			

Figure 3.2   Daily Planner

Date:_____

| Priorities: | Accomplished | Notes: |

1._____ ☐ _____
2._____ ☐ _____
3._____ ☐ _____
4._____ ☐ _____
5._____ ☐ _____
6._____ ☐ _____
7._____ ☐ _____
8._____ ☐ _____
9._____ ☐ _____
10._____ ☐ _____

	Contacts	Qualified Leads	Listing Appointments	Showings
Activity				

	Listings Obtained	Sales	Listings Sold
Results			

Figure 3.2   Daily Planner

Date:_____

Priorities: Accomplished   Notes:

1._____   ❑   _____
2._____   ❑   _____
3._____   ❑   _____
4._____   ❑   _____
5._____   ❑   _____
6._____   ❑   _____
7._____   ❑   _____
8._____   ❑   _____
9._____   ❑   _____
10._____ ❑   _____

	Contacts	Qualified Leads	Listing Appointments	Showings
Activity				

	Listings Obtained	Sales	Listings Sold
Results			

Figure 3.2　Daily Planner

Date:_____

Priorities:		Accomplished	Notes:

1._____　☐　_____
2._____　☐　_____
3._____　☐　_____
4._____　☐　_____
5._____　☐　_____
6._____　☐　_____
7._____　☐　_____
8._____　☐　_____
9._____　☐　_____
10._____　☐　_____

	Contacts	Qualified Leads	Listing Appointments	Showings
Activity				

	Listings Obtained	Sales	Listings Sold
Results			

Figure 3.2 Daily Planner

Date:_____

Priorities: Accomplished   Notes:

1._____   ☐   _____
2._____   ☐   _____
3._____   ☐   _____
4._____   ☐   _____
5._____   ☐   _____
6._____   ☐   _____
7._____   ☐   _____
8._____   ☐   _____
9._____   ☐   _____
10._____   ☐   _____

	Contacts	Qualified Leads	Listing Appointments	Showings
Activity				

	Listings Obtained	Sales	Listings Sold
Results			

Figure 3.2   Daily Planner

Date:_____

| Priorities: | Accomplished | Notes: |

Priorities: Accomplished   Notes:

1._____   ☐   _____

2._____   ☐   _____

3._____   ☐   _____

4._____   ☐   _____

5._____   ☐   _____

6._____   ☐   _____

7._____   ☐   _____

8._____   ☐   _____

9._____   ☐   _____

10._____   ☐   _____

	Contacts	Qualified Leads	Listing Appointments	Showings
Activity				

	Listings Obtained	Sales	Listings Sold
Results			

Figure 3.3   Week One: Accomplishments

Business Development

Assignments	Completed	Manager's Comments
30 Days to Dollars **Activities** (Figure 11.3)	_____	_____
From Your Scorecard (Figure 11.4)	_____	_____
Buyers	_____	_____
Qualified Buyers:_____	_____	_____
Buyer Tours:_____	_____	_____
Sales:_____	_____	_____
Sellers		
Qualified Listing Presentations:_____	_____	_____
Qualified Listings:_____	_____	_____
Listings Sold:_____	_____	_____

Buyer/seller qualifiers in Section 9 have been completed:_____

Business Support

Assignments	Completed	Manager's Comments
	_____	_____
	_____	_____
	_____	_____
Preparations for Reactive Activities	_____	_____
	_____	_____
	_____	_____
	_____	_____
	_____	_____

Take these numbers from your grids (see Figures 11.3 and 11.4). The numbers you create will form the basis for your analysis of your personal ratios of calls to leads to appointments to sales. By keeping these numbers, you are becoming an effective manager of your own business-development program.

Weekly Activity Plan

Using the weekly planner (see Figure 3.1), plan your first week. Create your plan in the following order:

1. Log in office-scheduled events (e.g., office meeting, tour).
2. Log in assignments from office (e.g., floor time, open house).
3. Log in meeting with manager.
4. Log in business-producing activities/those on the business cycle (e.g., showings, listing presentations, writing offers).
5. Log in business-development activities (list prospecting first).
6. Log in support activities (including inspecting inventory and support assignments given here)

Example: See Joan Smith's plan for Week One in Section 10.

Your Daily Plan

Now, prioritize your activities for the week, and place them in your daily plan (see Figure 3.2). Six daily plans are included in each week's Section. In your daily planner, log in your sales accomplishments. Each day, when you accomplish your goals, give yourself a pat on the back.

Business Development

Using the *30 Days to Dollars* format discussed in Section 1, start prospecting. Begin with the best category—people you know. Complete the following activities:

- *Make a list of at least 100 people you could ask for a lead.* (See Section 7 and Section 8 for information on how to call on these people and listen to the audiotape for Week One.)
- *Using Sales Skill 1, craft a sales script to call on people you know.* (See Sections 7 and 8 for information about this sales skill.)
- *Using Sales Skill 2, attach a benefit* to them. (See Sections 7 and 8 for information about this sales skill.)
- *Using Sales Skill 3, ask for a lead.* (See Sections 7 and 8 for information about this sales skill.)
- *Call or see at least 50 people this week, and ask for a lead* using the three new sales skills.

Start your *circle prospecting*. Choose an area to circle prospect in and a home to circle prospect around. (See Section 7 for more information on circle prospecting. Listen to the audiotape for Week One for the system and dialogue.)

- Craft a sales call for circle prospecting using all three new sales skills.
- Circle prospect at least 50 homes. Ask for a lead.

Achieve the following results from your prospecting (log the qualified buyers and sellers in the grids in Section 9):

- Secure two qualified buyer leads.
- Secure two qualified seller leads.
- Put customers in the car at least twice.
- Schedule and give one listing presentation.

Before beginning your Week One assignments, log in your prospecting and results goals for the week on your grids in Section 11. Each day, log in your "actuals," and tally them at the end of the week. Carry your goals and actuals to Week One: Accomplishment (see Figure 3.3), and log them in. Compare goals with actuals.

Business Support

Become comfortable with the operation of the office. Ask your manager or office manager for an orientation checklist. Read the office operations manual, if one is available. Become acquainted with all support materials.

Learn the basics of financing and qualifying. Meet with a loan officer. Set as many appointments as you wish with the loan officer until you are comfortable with the basics.

Complete a market analysis on your own home. Package it. Practice your presentation of your market analysis. Inspect three agents' market analyses, and include their best points in your package. Create three visual methods to counter sellers' objections to pricing.

Preparation for Reactive Prospecting Activities

Most offices provide scheduling for two *reactive* prospecting activities (the agent waits for a prospect to come to him):

1. Floor time
2. Public open houses

Plan for no more than 20 percent of your leads to come from reactive activities!

To prepare to start these activities:

- *Observe two different people holding floor time in your office.* Inspect the resource materials available. Gather information on how agents handle the calls and objections. How do they get the phone number? Find any resources (e.g., articles, books, audiotapes) in your office that show you how to handle floor calls. Practice getting the appointment with a friend. Role play various sales situations.

- *Observe ten public open houses this weekend.* Make notes on the strategies that you think are good; those that are bad. Interview three agents on how they prepare for and hold open houses. Learn five strategies that they use to control the prospect to get an appointment.

Final Thoughts for Week One

If you're like many new agents, at the end of Week One, your brain feels like mush. New words, new systems, unfamiliar territory—it's no wonder that, after the first week, new agents reevaluate their "charge ahead" attitude and decide to ease into the career! They reason that, instead of talking to people so quickly, they must spend more time on learning, in research, in organization. Why? The bravado and excitement of starting a new career fades as these new agents face the realities of rejections. Their confidence decreases as rejection increases. New agents conclude that, to increase their confidence, they need more knowledge. A little of that's okay. But, be careful.

Accumulating knowledge can become a vicious cycle—the more knowledge you have, the more you want to give to those you meet. Remember the difference between social communication and sales communication? Becoming knowledgeable and dumping it on unsuspecting strangers merely means the strangers get and maintain control.

Building Real, Lasting Confidence

Up and Running is designed to build your confidence the right way—through increasing your skills. Why? Because real estate is a performance art, not a knowledge pursuit. True confidence in real estate is built from successful performance. As a pianist, I know that my confidence level is highest right after a good performance. In fact, the performers I know say that, after a successful performance, they want to go right out and play that number again! Great performance is the *best* motivator. However, until I perform, I have only my practice and imagination to build my confidence. Although there are methods to increase your confidence mentally, they pale before the reality of a great performance.

Next Best Thing Is Practice

It's painful to learn from your mistakes with real customers. However, there's another effective way to learn skills—practice. In my experience, real estate agents and managers really underestimate the value of *practice.* How do you practice? By role-playing each segment that requires sales communication with people:

- Prospecting scenarios
- Counseling/qualifying buyer scenarios
- Showing and closing buyer scenarios
- Presenting and negotiating offer scenarios
- Qualifying seller scenarios
- Marketing presentation scenarios
- Price reduction/review scenarios

Agents believe that, since they can talk, they can sell. But, we've already discussed the realities of conversation versus the special communication skills required for sales success. I guarantee that, if you take seriously the practice asked of you in *Up and Running,* your performance with people will improve quickly. And your confidence will soar. Every successful salesperson I've known who started quickly in this business practiced, organized, systematized and perfected each step in the sales cycle.

Perfect Practice Makes Perfect

The best kind of practice quickly increases your skill and results. Back to my piano-practicing days: As a four-year-old, I picked out tunes on the keys and added the chords. I could play pop music reasonably well. Then, at age six, I started piano lessons. As I progressed to more demanding piano teachers, I learned that "faking it till you made it" just would not meet their standards. In fact, my best piano teacher, Mr. Green, taught me to practice very slowly, so *there weren't any mistakes.* I found, that, if I practiced quickly, I practiced my mistakes right along with the rest of the piece!

Although practice was tedious, using Mr. Green's method, I became a much better pianist. Too often, real estate agents practice the mistakes and end up with a sales system that is "more mistake than effective."

Thus, to optimize your practice, practice perfectly. *Perfect practice makes perfect.*

A Desire To Do It Again

If you have ever experienced the exhilaration of a fine performance, you know what I mean when I say that you want to run right out and do it again! Success is a great motivator. As we progress throughout these four weeks of business-producing assignments, we will be discussing self-motivation. But for now, let's just say that good performance is the best motivator. And, very simply, the best motivator for selling is *selling*. This is the greatest reason to get out into the field, even before you're comfortable—to motivate yourself to continue in your quest for a successful real estate career.

Week Two

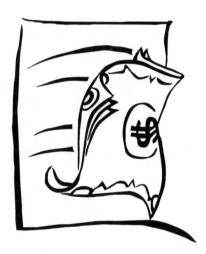

This week you will continue the business-producing activities introduced in Week One, and you will add one additional type of prospecting. Even though you may choose not to use some of the prospecting methods introduced here long term, you are expanding your skills. You are developing a prospecting repertoire. When I was in college, I worked my way through school playing piano in bars. I found that the more tunes and styles I could play, the more tips I made. Hence, I developed a wide repertoire. I never knew when it would come in handy. Having several prospecting skills available to you is your insurance plan against changing markets.

Besides learning some new sales skills in Week Two, you will start assembling your systems for controlling buyers and sellers.

Objectives

Business Development

- Continue *30 Days to Dollars* prospecting, adding one additional type of prospecting.
- Make 100 sales calls using the categories in *30 Days to Dollars*.
- Get two qualified showing appointments.
- Get one qualified listing appointment.
- Apply two new sales skills.

Business Support

- Assemble listing presentation materials.
- Assemble counseling packet for buyers, and buyer strategies.
- Write two purchase and sale agreements for practice.
- Begin contact management system for prospects.
- Become proficient at prospecting skills in the categories added.
- Practice two new sales skills.

Weekly Activity Plan

Create your weekly plan, following the guidelines in Week One. Using Figure 4.1, log in your activities in the same order. Then, prioritize your weekly plan. Using Figure 4.2, log your prioritized activities into each of your daily plans. Following this same format for one month will create a success-building habit. You will never be the kind of agent who sits around the office waiting for someone to plan for you. As you accomplish your goals, log them into your Week Two: Accomplishments (see Figure 4.3).

Figure 4.1   Your Weekly Plan

Name: _____

Week: _____

Time	Monday	Tuesday	Wednesday	Thursday	Friday	Saturday	Sunday
7–8							
8–9							
9–10							
10–11							
11–12							
12–1							
1–2							
2–3							
3–4							
4–5							
5–6							
6–7							
7–8							
8–9							

Figure 4.2 Daily Planner

Date:_____

Priorities: Accomplished   Notes:

1._____   ☐   _____
2._____   ☐   _____
3._____   ☐   _____
4._____   ☐   _____
5._____   ☐   _____
6._____   ☐   _____
7._____   ☐   _____
8._____   ☐   _____
9._____   ☐   _____
10._____   ☐   _____

	Contacts	Qualified Leads	Listing Appointments	Showings
Activity				

	Listings Obtained	Sales	Listings Sold
Results			

Figure 4.2   Daily Planner

Date:_____

Priorities: Accomplished   Notes:

1._____ ☐ _____
2._____ ☐ _____
3._____ ☐ _____
4._____ ☐ _____
5._____ ☐ _____
6._____ ☐ _____
7._____ ☐ _____
8._____ ☐ _____
9._____ ☐ _____
10._____ ☐ _____

	Contacts	Qualified Leads	Listing Appointments	Showings
Activity				

	Listings Obtained	Sales	Listings Sold
Results			

Figure 4.2   Daily Planner

Date:_____

Priorities: Accomplished   Notes:

1._____   ☐   _____

2._____   ☐   _____

3._____   ☐   _____

4._____   ☐   _____

5._____   ☐   _____

6._____   ☐   _____

7._____   ☐   _____

8._____   ☐   _____

9._____   ☐   _____

10._____   ☐   _____

	Contacts	Qualified Leads	Listing Appointments	Showings
Activity				

	Listings Obtained	Sales	Listings Sold
Results			

Figure 4.2   Daily Planner

Date:_____

Priorities:	Accomplished	Notes:
1._____	☐	_____
2._____	☐	_____
3._____	☐	_____
4._____	☐	_____
5._____	☐	_____
6._____	☐	_____
7._____	☐	_____
8._____	☐	_____
9._____	☐	_____
10._____	☐	_____

	Contacts	Qualified Leads	Listing Appointments	Showings
Activity				

	Listings Obtained	Sales	Listings Sold
Results			

Figure 4.2 Daily Planner

Date:_____

Priorities:	Accomplished	Notes:

1._____ ☐ _____

2._____ ☐ _____

3._____ ☐ _____

4._____ ☐ _____

5._____ ☐ _____

6._____ ☐ _____

7._____ ☐ _____

8._____ ☐ _____

9._____ ☐ _____

10._____ ☐ _____

	Contacts	Qualified Leads	Listing Appointments	Showings
Activity				

	Listings Obtained	Sales	Listings Sold
Results			

Figure 4.2   Daily Planner

Date:_____

Priorities: Accomplished   Notes:

1._____ ☐ _____

2._____ ☐ _____

3._____ ☐ _____

4._____ ☐ _____

5._____ ☐ _____

6._____ ☐ _____

7._____ ☐ _____

8._____ ☐ _____

9._____ ☐ _____

10._____ ☐ _____

	Contacts	Qualified Leads	Listing Appointments	Showings
Activity				

	Listings Obtained	Sales	Listings Sold
Results			

Figure 4.3   Week Two: Accomplishments

Business Development

Assignments	Completed	Manager's Comments
30 Days to Dollars **Activities** (Figure 11.3)	_____	_____
From Your Scorecard (Figure 11.4)	_____	_____
Buyers	_____	_____
Qualified Buyers:_____	_____	_____
Buyer Tours:_____	_____	_____
Sales:_____	_____	_____
Sellers		
Qualified Listing Presentations:_____	_____	_____
Qualified Listings:_____	_____	_____
Listings Sold:_____	_____	_____

Buyer/seller qualifiers in Section 9 have been completed:_____

Business Support

Assignments	Completed	Manager's Comments
	_____	_____
	_____	_____
	_____	_____
	_____	_____
	_____	_____
	_____	_____
	_____	_____
	_____	_____

Take these numbers from your grids (see Figures 11.3 and 11.4). The numbers you create will form the basis for your analysis of your personal ratios of calls to leads to appointments to sales. By keeping these numbers, you are becoming an effective manager of your own business-development program.

Business Development

Continue the *30 Days to Dollars* plan discussed in Section 1 with the following activities:

- Call on at least 25 people you know. Ask for leads.
- Circle prospect at least 50 homes. Ask for leads.
- Call on 25 for-sale-by-owners or expired listings.

Listen to the audiotape for Week Two, and refer to Sections 7 and 8 for additional information on these prospecting methods.

Hold one public open house this weekend. To prepare and get the best strategies, talk to three people in your office. (This is a reactive strategy. However, you will get leads by calling on the homeowners around this home prior to the open house, or circle prospecting.)

Continue using Sales Skills 1, 2 and 3 (see Sections 7 and 8) as you prospect and work with buyers and sellers. Add Sales Skill 4: Objection-Busters—Using the AAA Method. (Listen to the audiotapes for Week Two and refer to Sections 7 and 8 in this book for more information.) Craft an *objection-buster* to the three common objections you get when you are prospecting. Practice answering these objections using the AAA method (see Sections 7 and 8). Use this method to counter your three most common objections as you prospect this week.

Before beginning your Week Two business-developing activities, log in your goals (see Figures 11.3 and 11.4).

From prospecting, you should strive to get the following results:

- Two qualified buyer appointments
- Two showing appointments with buyers
- Two qualified seller leads
- One qualified listing presentation

If you do not get these results from your prospecting, increase the numbers of calls you're making.

Log your qualified buyers and sellers into your grids (see Figures 9.1, 9.2, 9.3 and 9.4) Be sure these people are qualified, so that you aren't wasting your time.

Business Support

Clarify the portions and systems in your listing process. Review the pattern of the listing process (from your initial training program or from interviewing agents in your office). Gather the materials for this whole listing process. Decide which materials to use for your first visit, the marketing part of your presentation and your pricing presentation.

Review three agents' presentations. Take notes on the strategies you want to incorporate, and assemble your listing process materials.

Using Sales Skill 4: The AAA method to craft objection-busters, practice answering three common seller objections to listing with you. Create three visuals to substantiate your information.

Clarify and assemble the portions and systems of the buying process. Interview three agents on the process and materials they use to counsel and qualify a buyer prior to putting the buyer in the car. (Include a strategy and materials on asking for a buyers' loyalty, as well as a discussion and materials concerning Agency disclosure.) Assemble these materials into a buyer's packet—a professional resource for helping a buyer through the buying process. (See the *List the Buyer System*, which gives detailed information on this package.)

Using Sales Skill 4, interview the agents on the three most common objections buyers have to buying, and how these agents handle those objections. Using the AAA method to crafting objection-busters, craft your strategy for handling these objections. Create three visuals you'll need to substantiate your claims.

Write two purchase and sale agreements. Practice writing purchase and sale agreements, so that you will be comfortable writing the actual agreements. Include a practice agreement for purchasing the property you currently own, and one using a method to purchase other than conventional financing.

Create your contact management system. Investigate and organize your contact management system. Interview three agents to learn how they organize their prospects, customers and clients. Decide on a system (manual or computer), and start it this week.

Final Thoughts for Week Two

If you have been prospecting consistently, you have probably found some buyers to qualify. Hopefully, you have even shown houses to a few buyers this week. On the listing side, you have no doubt found at least one homeowner who was interested in selling his or her home. You have made one listing presentation. As the list grows and opportunities increase, you begin to experience some *time management* challenges. To help you manage your time, try the solutions recommended in the following paragraphs.

Continue Your Weekly Plan

It's amazing how many agents don't plan their week—ahead of their week! In fact, from teaching sales skill workshops, I found that less than ten percent of experienced agents actually lay out a week's work in advance. When they look at what they accomplished the prior month, they're stunned. From analyzing their prior month's activities, they discover that they have been nonproductive because they:

- let nonincome-producing activities dominate their schedule;
- allowed well-meaning people to steal their time; and
- put too much emphasis on support activities.

They became their own assistants! However, with new insights, agents can get back on track and create a plan that helps them reach their goals. *Up and Running* teaches you, from the beginning, how to prioritize your activities so that you can avoid this common mistake.

Don't Stop Prospecting

There's one sure way to create a low-producing career: Stop prospecting when you are busy with other activities. As my friend Bill Feldman says, "When you stop pedaling the bicycle, you fall off." Pedaling the bicycle fast enough to stay on track simply means planning, executing and monitoring your business-developing plan (prospecting) to provide you with enough new leads to give you the results that will meet your goals.

Following the Leader—Who's the Leader? How much money do you think, on average, a REALTOR® makes? According to surveys, the public thinks agents make about $50,000. Actually, it's about half that—less than $25,000, which in most areas translates to about 13 transactions a year. (That's for all REALTORS®, regardless of the number of years they have been in the business.) Is that more or less than you expect of yourself in your first year? The point is this: If you expect to complete more than 12 transactions your first year, do not follow the example of most real estate agents.

Who have you modeled your weekly plan after? Be sure it's a producer who has attained to your own expectations. If not, you'll find yourself unwittingly performing many support activities, drinking coffee, gossiping and *not* creating a successful real estate career.

Ask Yourself: What Do I Need To Do To Get into Action?

Accumulating knowledge as a confidence builder is a common mistake new agents make. Ned was an example of this. In the business eight months, Ned had earned $2,000. He was in the office regularly and appeared busy with paperwork. He attended law courses and was well-informed on financing. One day I saw Ned collating maps. I asked him what he was doing. He explained that he was putting together a series of maps for a buyer's tour. I thought that was exceptional; buyers would really want to know the whereabouts of the homes they were seeing. Unfortunately, Ned had used his strategy with only two buyers—that's all the buyers he had put in his car in the past three months! He had spent his time on this nifty map system, but had not talked to enough people to get them into the car—or have the opportunity to appreciate the map system! Which is more important to your goal attainment? Talking to people, qualifying them and showing them homes, or working diligently on a map system (so you will be prepared) in case you find someone who wants you to show them homes?

How Do You "Get into Action"?   In a wonderful book, *The Conative Connection*, Kathy Kolbe explores the ways different personalities get into action—not how we *learn,* but how we *get into action.* Some people (like me) barge ahead and worry about the details later. We start badly, but, because we're tenacious, we surprise people by how good we finally get. Unfortunately, our supervisors often remember only how bad we were when we started. We must be tough-minded and keep at it; we must retain an image of ourselves as "finished products," because others will not see us that way. Other people, like my son, observe the action for a long time. Finally, when they feel ready to perform well, they get into action. They start slowly but well. Because of their slow start, they don't get much positive reinforcement from their supervisor (or coach or manager), who notes their lack of progress compared to others in the office. If these slow starters are tenacious and believe in themselves, they become very good because they practice perfectly. Kolbe, in her book, points out several "get into action" styles. How do you get into action? This book will help you to pinpoint the barriers and challenges you face as you start your real estate career.

Go Ahead. Be Embarrassed.   From my description of my "get into action" mode, you can see that "go ahead, be embarrassed" is my admittedly biased way of saying "just do it." There's no way to be experienced until you get experience. No agent likes to take risks, to be embarrassed, to have buyers and sellers guess that he or she is new in the business. But let's face it—everyone has been new in the business. Just go ahead and get those first few "new" months over with. You will be embarrassed every day—many times. As a new agent, my most common statement to buyers or sellers was: "I don't know, but I'll find out." I came from the musical field; I had a Master's degree. I had been "tickling the ivories" since I was four years old. In music little could stump me. But in real estate anything could stump me! However, I muddled through it, and you will, too. I didn't have *Up and Running* or the excellent training programs offered by companies today to get me started. You, on the other hand, have many advantages.

Taking Your Time.   I wish I could tell you that you can successfully launch your real estate career by taking lots of time to "get ready." However, if you take all the time in the world, you will fail for three reasons:

1. *Real estate is a performance art.* It doesn't matter how much you know; it only matters how you interact with people. And that takes practice. In the performance field, we know that, to remember and emulate good performance, we need to perform right after we have heard, seen and practiced that performance. Learning something in a class and letting that skill lie dormant for months just guarantees poor skill—and high stress.

2. *The only true motivator is selling.* Tell me that you're in no hurry, that you have plenty of time to make your first sale. I'll predict, that, within three months, you'll be mentally, if not physically, out of real estate. Why? Because it's tough to stay motivated without some positive reinforcement. The longer it takes you to make a sale, the more reasons you will find to leave the business.

3. *Your mentors, your manager and perhaps your adviser will lose interest in you.*   Since they don't see you taking meaningful action steps, your mentors will naturally become less motivated to help you. For you to stay motivated, you need the positive support of your mentors. How long does it take for managers and mentors to lose interest in a new agent? From my experience, it takes about two months. If I don't see a lot of prospecting and working with people within that first two months, I turn my attention to other agents who are creating activities. It's difficult and time-consuming to constantly think of new ways to motivate agents after they are deflated—again!

Straight Ahead and Strive for Tone

This old musical saying aptly describes what I mean. At the beginning of your career, doing it is more important than preparing to do it—or knowing about it. Do it the best you can—and you'll learn how to do it better. Now, let's move on to your third week in the business!

Week Three

This week, again, you will add to your prospecting and sales skill repertoire. To gain confidence in purchase and sale agreements, you will write some agreements using different methods of financing. To increase your credibility with buyers and sellers, make these exercises challenging.

Even though you are new in the business, now is the time to set yourself apart from the crowd. You will begin this process in this week's assignments.

Objectives

Business Development

- Complete 100 sales calls, including using one new contact method.
- Get two qualified buyer leads.
- Get two qualified seller leads.
- Show homes to two qualified buyer groups.
- Attend two listing appointments.
- List one marketable property.
- Apply one new sales skill.

Business Support

- Learn two methods of writing purchase and sale agreements, using alternative methods of financing, including one offer contingent on the sale of the purchaser's home.
- Create personal promotion pieces, including a professional portfolio (agent promotional brochure, or "friendly" resume). See the References section for information on assembling a portfolio.
- Create a follow-up plan that ties into a contact management plan for recontacting leads to date.
- Gain performance excellence with Sales Skill 5.
- Create performance excellence in handling objections through crafting three more objection-busters with visuals.

Weekly Activity Plan

Create your weekly plan, following the guidelines in Week One. Using Figure 5.1, prioritize your activities. Log them into your daily planners (see Figure 5.2). Set your goals, and keep track of your "actuals" in Section 11. Record your accomplishments for this week in Figure 5.3.

Figure 5.1 Your Weekly Plan

Week: _____

Name: _____

Time	Monday	Tuesday	Wednesday	Thursday	Friday	Saturday	Sunday
7–8							
8–9							
9–10							
10–11							
11–12							
12–1							
1–2							
2–3							
3–4							
4–5							
5–6							
6–7							
7–8							
8–9							

Figure 5.2   Daily Planner

Date:_____

Priorities:	Accomplished	Notes:
1._____	☐	_____
2._____	☐	_____
3._____	☐	_____
4._____	☐	_____
5._____	☐	_____
6._____	☐	_____
7._____	☐	_____
8._____	☐	_____
9._____	☐	_____
10._____	☐	_____

	Contacts	Qualified Leads	Listing Appointments	Showings
Activity				

	Listings Obtained	Sales	Listings Sold
Results			

Figure 5.2   Daily Planner

Date:_____

Priorities:	Accomplished	Notes:
1._____	☐	_____
2._____	☐	_____
3._____	☐	_____
4._____	☐	_____
5._____	☐	_____
6._____	☐	_____
7._____	☐	_____
8._____	☐	_____
9._____	☐	_____
10._____	☐	_____

	Contacts	Qualified Leads	Listing Appointments	Showings
Activity				

	Listings Obtained	Sales	Listings Sold
Results			

Figure 5.2 Daily Planner

Date:_____

Priorities: Accomplished   Notes:

1._____ ☐ _____
2._____ ☐ _____
3._____ ☐ _____
4._____ ☐ _____
5._____ ☐ _____
6._____ ☐ _____
7._____ ☐ _____
8._____ ☐ _____
9._____ ☐ _____
10._____ ☐ _____

	Contacts	Qualified Leads	Listing Appointments	Showings
Activity				

	Listings Obtained	Sales	Listings Sold
Results			

Figure 5.2 Daily Planner

Date:_____

Priorities: Accomplished   Notes:

1._____ ☐ _____
2._____ ☐ _____
3._____ ☐ _____
4._____ ☐ _____
5._____ ☐ _____
6._____ ☐ _____
7._____ ☐ _____
8._____ ☐ _____
9._____ ☐ _____
10._____ ☐ _____

	Contacts	Qualified Leads	Listing Appointments	Showings
Activity				

	Listings Obtained	Sales	Listings Sold
Results			

Figure 5.2   Daily Planner

Date:_____

Priorities: Accomplished   Notes:

1._____ ☐ _____
2._____ ☐ _____
3._____ ☐ _____
4._____ ☐ _____
5._____ ☐ _____
6._____ ☐ _____
7._____ ☐ _____
8._____ ☐ _____
9._____ ☐ _____
10._____ ☐ _____

	Contacts	Qualified Leads	Listing Appointments	Showings
Activity				

	Listings Obtained	Sales	Listings Sold
Results			

Figure 5.2   Daily Planner

Date:_____

Priorities: Accomplished   Notes:

1._____ ☐ _____
2._____ ☐ _____
3._____ ☐ _____
4._____ ☐ _____
5._____ ☐ _____
6._____ ☐ _____
7._____ ☐ _____
8._____ ☐ _____
9._____ ☐ _____
10._____ ☐ _____

	Contacts	Qualified Leads	Listing Appointments	Showings
Activity				

	Listings Obtained	Sales	Listings Sold
Results			

Figure 5.3   Week Three: Accomplishments

Business Development

Assignments	Completed	Manager's Comments
30 Days to Dollars **Activities** (Figure 11.3)	_____	_____
From Your Scorecard (Figure 11.4)	_____	_____
Buyers	_____	_____
Qualified Buyers:_____	_____	_____
Buyer Tours:_____	_____	_____
Sales:_____	_____	_____
Sellers		
Qualified Listing Presentations:_____	_____	_____
Qualified Listings:_____	_____	_____
Listings Sold:_____	_____	_____

Buyer/seller qualifiers in Section 9 have been completed:_____

Business Support

Assignments	Completed	Manager's Comments
	_____	_____
	_____	_____
	_____	_____
	_____	_____
	_____	_____
	_____	_____
	_____	_____
	_____	_____

Translate these numbers to your grids (see Figures 11.3 and 11.4), so that you can start your own self-management program. The numbers you create will form the basis for your analysis of your personal ratios of calls to leads to appointments to sales. By keeping these numbers, you are becoming the master of your own business-development program.

Business Development

Make 100 sales calls, using the *30 Days to Dollars* priorities of target markets and numbers. Choose the markets you will call on. Make the second call to the for-sale-by-owners or expired listings that you began last week.

Strive to achieve the following business-development results:

- Get two qualified buyer appointments.
- Show homes to two qualified buyer groups.
- Get two appointments to do a listing presentation.
- List one marketable property.

If your numbers of prospects are not providing the leads you need, increase your numbers of prospects. Log in your qualified buyers and sellers in the grids in Section 9.

Apply Sales Skill 5, the "hum technique." (Listen to the audiotape for Week Three and refer to Sections 7 and 8 for more information.) Use this technique in your prospecting and qualifying conversations with buyers and sellers.

Business Support

Create reasons for people to choose you. Substantiate them in writing. Prepare a professional portfolio or brochure to promote yourself. Ask three agents in your office for ideas on promotional pieces and/or the portfolio.

Increase your skill with purchase and sale agreements. Write two purchase and sale agreements using alternative financing methods. Make one offer contingent on the sale of a purchaser's home. Check these offers with your manager to be sure that you are using all the wordings and addenda available to you.

Turn calls into leads through establishing a follow-up program. Create a follow-up plan for regularly re-communicating with your leads. Include in the plan when and how leads are contacted, script used, materials included and objective of the call. Note the dates to contact leads in your daily planner.

Final Thoughts for Week Three

By now, you should be developing the success habits that new agents need to ensure a fast-starting career. The exciting part—and the part you will not appreciate for another year—is that you have subconsciously created a job description that is different from most agents'. Your job description is centered around the business of real estate—not the research of real estate. Unfortunately, many agents start their real estate careers in a research mode—trying to find out all there is to know about the field. These agents become known for their knowledge. People compliment them on their understanding of finance and their accumulation of property information; people use this information. Since it's human nature for people to continue what they get rewarded or complimented for, these agents continue accumulating knowledge!

Be Certain about What You Want

You are learning good habits that lead to creating a productive business. You are correctly prioritizing your activities in order to build the right job description. Continue these success habits, and you will become known as a salesperson.

It's easy to slip into a different job description and become known for something other than production. John was an agent in the first office I managed. When I was still working as an agent, I admired John's depth of information about waterfront property and asked him to share his information with me. John was happy to help me out. I realized that John wasn't very successful, yet I considered that his business. Later, when I became manager of the office, I discovered that John was completing only six transactions a year—in his third year in the business—not enough to continuously build his business or support our office image as full-time committed professionals. Yet John, who had received positive reinforcement for his *knowledge,* was content. Since we established standards of excellence in our office (which included production minimums), it was my job as a manager to work with John to help him increase his production. Working together, John and I agreed that, for him to stay with our office, he would have to change his job description. This, admittedly, would be difficult, because he had been encouraged to sustain his reputation as *a waterfront expert.* In fact, it proved impossible—John liked the comfort of collating more than the excitement of selling real estate.

Create the Future—Your Way

You have been in the business three weeks. How do you see yourself? Is your image of yourself different from the one you had when you started in this business? Successful performers have learned to create a "completed" picture of themselves as great performers—*long before they* are *terrific performers.* This helps them to predict the outcome of their efforts. If you don't know where you're going, you can't get there!

Lou Tice, the founder of Pacific Institute, calls this skill *self-efficacy.* It is the ability to create yourself as a finished "product" in your head and hold that image, even though no one in the outside world has a clue that you are going to end up that way. What a skill! This technique is practiced in the sports world. When our son, Chris, took karate lessons he learned this skill of self-efficacy. First, he watched great performers—black belts—performing the *katas* (fighting moves in a format) and *kumite* (actual fighting). Then he envisioned himself performing each part of these moves. He put the complete picture together. Finally, he performed the moves, very slowly, *practicing perfectly.* He was coached every step of the way to ensure that he was practicing perfectly. After he perfected each move in context, he practiced performing faster. This method of creating perfect performance resulted in Chris's winning several medals in national and international competition—even while he was going through great growth spurts. His developed skill of self-efficacy ensured that his mind would hold the picture of his perfect performance. This skill has proved to be an invaluable asset throughout his life.

Develop the Professional "You"

Take a few minutes in a quiet place by yourself. Imagine yourself as the successful real estate agent you intend to be. What will you do? Say? What will people say about you? What kind of recognition will you get? What affiliations will you make that reflect your ideal of yourself as a pro? What power will you have? Create a movie with you as the star, complete with the movement, color, dialogue, tastes and smells. Make it fun, exciting and rewarding. Make it in Technicolor. Now, play it over and over in your head—20 times a day for a month. Why? To counteract your "growth spurts" (e.g., objections, barriers, negative self-talk, lost leads) as you start your career. You must develop some *mental ammunition.* Remember, people treat you as they see you. They can't see the new movie that you created until you start acting it out. Even then, they will try to put you back into your "old movie." Why? Because it's human nature. In our office, we knew John as a waterfront collator, not a salesperson. Unwittingly, we help our friends fail by not becoming supporting players in their new picture. You must have a strong movie to move yourself in the direction you want to go, so that others can get caught up in the new action and let go of the old. Tough-minded again, huh?

Show That You're the Professional of Choice

Recently, an agent who had been in the business about a year told me that she couldn't get people who came to her open houses to appreciate her belief that she could help them—if they could only get to know her. The reason she couldn't get them to appreciate her was that she didn't have time to engage them in conversation—to show them that she was knowledgeable and caring. Before she could talk to them, they were inching out the door. Her problem, stated in context of self-efficacy, was that she wasn't able to play her "movie as a pro" for people. But how could she? The public comes into open houses with three objectives:

1. To see the home
2. To get information
3. To avoid the salesperson

What does the public think about real estate salespeople? Generally, that one is as good as another. Do you believe that's true? How can customers differentiate you from any other agent as they visit open houses? In training courses, I ask agents how they are different from the public's general view of a real estate agent. The reply: "I'm an honest, enthusiastic, service-oriented, professional." Then I ask the students how they *demonstrate* these qualities. The reply: "I demonstrate my qualities through the way I act with buyers and sellers." Here's the problem. People attending an open house want to avoid you, not get to know you. They will not give you the time to see you in the actions that prove your qualities. Unless you can *quickly* show them you are a cut above the "generic" agent, they will attempt an escape, just as they have with the other ten agents whose homes they have visited.

Project the Professional "You"

How do professionals in other fields demonstrate their professional "selves"? Envision your doctor's office. On the walls are diplomas that give you confidence about the doctor's qualifications. How do restaurants demonstrate—*before you eat the food*—that their food and service is good? Reviews from the newspaper, testimonials from customers. You can inspire confidence in your services by adopting some of the same promotional strategies that successful professionals and businesses use. In this week's assignments, you were to start developing your professional portfolio. For detailed information about exactly how to develop and use this portfolio, refer to my handbook/tape set, *Developing a Portfolio That Sells You.* I recommend that you develop the portfolio. You will learn how to create a strong portfolio that will compete with any experienced agent's.

Project Your Movie—Increase Your Confidence

Developing a portfolio provides an additional benefit. During the development process, you complete exercises that help you develop your unique approach to the business. You draw on your particular strengths, services and business approaches that differentiate you from the "generic" agent. Then you project these in a pictorial way to communicate added value to the potential client or customer. The result is an overall promotional strategy that will compete successfully in the marketplace. The best news, for you, the new agent, is that this process helps develop your "movie" and greatly increases your confidence level.

As a new agent, I developed a portfolio that I used over a period of years. Now, as a manager, I have developed a manager's portfolio. I believe in this process and strategy so strongly that I created a product especially for managers. *The Recruiter* helps managers develop highly unique, creative, effective promotional strategies to differentiate them from the "generic" manager—and attract the recruits they really want.

Remember: It's not the finished portfolio, but the process of thinking through your strengths, challenges and competitors that is most important. Why? Because, in this highly competitive world of real estate sales and management, you must have a clearly, precisely defined picture of you as a "cut above." To compete you must create, define, refine and promote yourself masterfully. The bonus to you is that you will have created your "movie!" (For more about this movie concept, see my book, *The Real Estate Agent's Business Planning Guide*.) Then, when you are facing those barriers and losing the vividness of your movie, simply open your portfolio and remind yourself of the special qualities, strengths and behaviors that propelled you into this business.

Week Four

You are now approaching your final week in the *Up and Running* activity plan. This week you will continue making the sales calls to create early success. You will refine your sellers' and buyers' presentations. You will add to your portfolio. These systems should be on their way to being professional, polished and practiced by now. Why? To ensure your success at every point of contact. (Note: As a pro, you will always be refining and tinkering with your systems. The objective in the first month is to get them to the point where you can use them as presentation guides.)

Objectives

Business Development

- Make 100 sales calls, using the methods that have proved to be most successful for you.
- Get two qualified listing appointments.
- Get two qualified showing appointments.
- Sell one home.
- Apply two new sales skills.

Business Support

- Complete the entire listing-process materials, including a market analysis package. Include eight visuals to counter common listing objections.
- Review and complete your counseling packet for buyers, including visuals for countering buyers' eight most common objections.
- Complete your personal promotional materials—either a professional portfolio and/or your personal brochure.
- Gain performance excellence in two new sales skills.

Weekly Activity Plan

Create your weekly plan, using the guidelines in Week One activity assignment (see Figure 6.1). Log in your activities and successes in Figures 6.2 and 6.3.

Figure 6.1   Your Weekly Plan

Time	Monday	Tuesday	Wednesday	Thursday	Friday	Saturday	Sunday
7–8							
8–9							
9–10							
10–11							
11–12							
12–1							
1–2							
2–3							
3–4							
4–5							
5–6							
6–7							
7–8							
8–9							

Week: _____   Name: _____

Figure 6.2   Daily Planner

Date:_____

Priorities: Accomplished   Notes:

1._____ ☐   _____

2._____ ☐   _____

3._____ ☐   _____

4._____ ☐   _____

5._____ ☐   _____

6._____ ☐   _____

7._____ ☐   _____

8._____ ☐   _____

9._____ ☐   _____

10._____ ☐   _____

	Contacts	Qualified Leads	Listing Appointments	Showings
Activity				

	Listings Obtained	Sales	Listings Sold
Results			

Figure 6.2   Daily Planner

Date:_____

Priorities: Accomplished   Notes:

1._____   ❏   _____
2._____   ❏   _____
3._____   ❏   _____
4._____   ❏   _____
5._____   ❏   _____
6._____   ❏   _____
7._____   ❏   _____
8._____   ❏   _____
9._____   ❏   _____
10._____ ❏   _____

	Contacts	Qualified Leads	Listing Appointments	Showings
Activity				

	Listings Obtained	Sales	Listings Sold
Results			

Figure 6.2   Daily Planner

Date:_____

Priorities: Accomplished   Notes:

1._____ ☐   _____

2._____ ☐   _____

3._____ ☐   _____

4._____ ☐   _____

5._____ ☐   _____

6._____ ☐   _____

7._____ ☐   _____

8._____ ☐   _____

9._____ ☐   _____

10._____ ☐   _____

	Contacts	Qualified Leads	Listing Appointments	Showings
Activity				

	Listings Obtained	Sales	Listings Sold
Results			

Figure 6.2   Daily Planner

Date:_____

Priorities: Accomplished   Notes:

1._____ ☐   _____
2._____ ☐   _____
3._____ ☐   _____
4._____ ☐   _____
5._____ ☐   _____
6._____ ☐   _____
7._____ ☐   _____
8._____ ☐   _____
9._____ ☐   _____
10._____ ☐   _____

	Contacts	Qualified Leads	Listing Appointments	Showings
Activity				

	Listings Obtained	Sales	Listings Sold
Results			

Figure 6.2   Daily Planner

Date:_____

Priorities: Accomplished   Notes:

1._____   ❏   _____

2._____   ❏   _____

3._____   ❏   _____

4._____   ❏   _____

5._____   ❏   _____

6._____   ❏   _____

7._____   ❏   _____

8._____   ❏   _____

9._____   ❏   _____

10._____   ❏   _____

	Contacts	Qualified Leads	Listing Appointments	Showings
Activity				

	Listings Obtained	Sales	Listings Sold
Results			

Figure 6.2   Daily Planner

Date:_____

Priorities: Accomplished   Notes:

1._____ ☐ _____
2._____ ☐ _____
3._____ ☐ _____
4._____ ☐ _____
5._____ ☐ _____
6._____ ☐ _____
7._____ ☐ _____
8._____ ☐ _____
9._____ ☐ _____
10._____ ☐ _____

	Contacts	Qualified Leads	Listing Appointments	Showings
Activity				

	Listings Obtained	Sales	Listings Sold
Results			

Figure 6.3   Week Four: Accomplishments

Business Development

Assignments	Completed	Manager's Comments
***30 Days to Dollars* Activities** (Figure 11.3)	_____	_____
From Your Scorecard (Figure 11.4)	_____	_____
Buyers	_____	_____
Qualified Buyers:_____	_____	_____
Buyer Tours:_____	_____	_____
Sales:_____	_____	_____
Sellers		
Qualified Listing Presentations:_____	_____	_____
Qualified Listings:_____	_____	_____
Listings Sold:_____	_____	_____

Buyer/seller qualifiers in Section 9 have been completed:_____

Business Support

Assignments	Completed	Manager's Comments
	_____	_____
	_____	_____
	_____	_____
	_____	_____
	_____	_____
	_____	_____
	_____	_____
	_____	_____

Translate these numbers to your grids (see Figures 11.3 and 11.4), so that you can start your own self-management program. The numbers you create will form the basis for your analysis of your personal ratios of calls to leads to appointments to sales. By keeping these numbers, you are becoming the master of your own business-development program.

Business Development

Using the *30 Days to Dollars* plan, make 100 sales calls, using the methods that have proven most successful for you. Review the audiotapes and information in Sections 7 and 8 to sharpen your skills. Make the third call to the for-sale-by-owners or expired listings that you have contacted twice.

From your prospecting efforts, strive for the following results:

- Get two listing appointments with qualified sellers.
- Get two showing appointments with qualified buyers.
- Sell one home.

Apply Sales Skills 6 and 7 (see Section 8) as you work with buyers and sellers this week. Listen to the audiotape for Week Four and refer to Sections 7 and 8 in this book for more information.

Business Support

Refine and complete your listing process. Complete your entire listing process materials; include eight visuals to counter sellers' objections. Apply the AAA technique to objection-busters to use with your visuals.

Complete your personal promotion materials and plan. Complete your professional portfolio or personal brochure. Include a distribution plan for using these tools to promote yourself, to prospect and to keep in touch with your customers and clients.

Complete and systematize your buyer process. Review and complete your buyers' counseling packet. Include eight visuals to counter buyers' common objections.

Your Next Step

Congratulations! You have experienced your first four weeks in the business. Not only have you completed this program, you have formed the habits of successful self-management:

- Completing consistent, *high-number contacts* for prospects
- *Qualifying prospects* for time management and control of your career

- Applying *sales skills* to your sales cycle
- Creating *business-producing activities* in large numbers

You have organized the support systems to the business that allow you to move faster:

- *Listing process* systems
- *Market analysis* package
- Working knowledge of *purchase and sale agreements*
- System for *counseling/qualifying* buyers
- Follow-up and *contact management* system
- *Personal promotional* tools and plan

You have dramatically increased your sales skills. You have practiced and applied the Seven Critical Sales Skills to success, so that you can better help buyers and sellers.

What's the next step? Continue your business development plan, analyze it, make changes as needed and plan longer-term. To help you take your planning process to the next level, refer to my book, *The Real Estate Agent's Business Planning Guide.* It shows you how to budget, explains marketing programs, gives you dozens of personal marketing ideas and assists you as you become an experienced top producer.

Congratulations for completing a challenging yet rewarding system that will get you off to the start in your real estate career that you need to ensure success. Continue the habits that you have begun, and you will enjoy a high-producing, profitable, long-term career.

Getting Leads

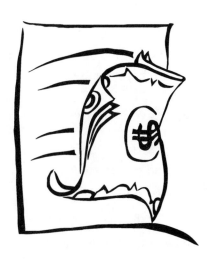

To get your business off to a quick start, you will want to go to the best sources for *leads*. To create your prospecting plan, follow these four principles of real estate marketing:

1. Segment your markets.
2. Be proactive.
3. Work the best sources.
4. Work the numbers.

Segment Markets

The population explosion, information overload—these and other cultural developments make it impossible to effectively promote yourself to everyone. To be an effective prospector today, you must *segment* and *prioritize* your potential markets. By segmenting your potential markets, you will discover certain best *targets*. A *target market* is a group of people defined through common demographics (i.e., age, income, real estate needs) and psychographics (i.e., lifestyle). In the '90s, to be an effective marketer, you need to clearly define your target markets and devise specific methods to sell to each. *30 Days to Dollars* segments markets and prioritizes them by *best sources of business*.

Be Proactive

To be successful in real estate today, you must get most of your business from *proactive prospecting* (you go out and meet people). *30 Days to Dollars* uses mainly proactive activities. There are two kinds of prospecting:

1. Proactive—you go out and find people
2. Reactive—you sit and wait for people

You can control the number of leads you can get (and the money you will make) through proactive methods.

Work the Best Sources

To be successful, you should start with your best sources of business. *30 Days to Dollars* prioritizes these sources for you.

Proactive sources include:

- Best—people you know
- Good—circle prospecting
- Immediate sources of listings:
  - For-sale-by-owners (FSBOs)
  - Expired listings
- Long-term—geographical farm

Reactive sources include:

- Open houses
- Floor time (This is not covered in *30 Days to Dollars*, since your office probably schedules floor time for you. To develop the special sales communication skills required to get appointments via the telephone, I suggest that you take a role-play oriented workshop in telephone techniques.)

Work the Numbers

To be an effective marketer, you must make enough calls to generate quality leads. *30 Days to Dollars* shows you which markets to target and how many calls you need to make—overall, 100 sales calls per week to ensure success—one sale and one listing in your first 30 days in the business.

How To Get Leads

This section shows you exactly how to make the sales call in each of the target markets in *30 Days to Dollars*. The audiotapes further explain these calls and provide role-plays so that you can hear the "script."

There are literally thousands of ways to make sales calls and to follow up. The best way is the one that works for you. How will you find out? Start with one method, then make adjustments for your style and market area. Is there a best way? Yes. *The best way is simply to get out into the field and start.*

As you learn to make these calls, you will practice and apply sales skills. These sales skills are referred to in your weekly assignments. The "how to" of these skills are found in Sections 7 and 8, as well as on the audiotapes.

Practice makes perfect. Before you make a sales call, "craft" your sales approach, using the sales skills described on the following pages. But, before you actually apply the sales skill in person, practice them with your manager, a fellow agent or your spouse, friend or child. Why? Because they will provide valuable feedback to help you be more effective in your actual sales calls.

Best Sources of Business: People You Know

To *craft a sales call* (Sales Skill 1, to be applied in Week One), use the following technique:

* Think of a particular person to call.
* Determine a potential real estate need and *benefit* (Sales Skill 2, to be applied in Week One) to this person.
* To discover these needs, write three questions to ask the person.

- Determine your *call objective.*
- Write a *question to get a lead* (Sales Skill 3, to be applied in Week One) or appointment—meet your objective.
- Write an opening statement.

This method of crafting calls works for crafting any initial sales call. For example:

- Joe Smith is a family friend.
- A potential real estate need and benefit to Joe is a rental home, which will reduce his tax burden.
- Three questions to ask:
  1. Is the equity in your present home enough to get a second mortgage to refinance for money to buy another home?
  2. Have you thought about reducing your tax burden?
  3. Have you looked into purchasing a home as a rental?
- The *call objective* is to get an appointment.
- The question to get the appointment is: When can we explore this potential?
- The opening statement is: I have been thinking about you. I'm in real estate now, and I have been exploring how to help people ease financial burdens with real estate.

Advanced Techniques

Accept the first no, and have the next question ready. With people you know, ask: Since I'm starting my real estate career, could I count on you to refer me to those who want to buy or sell? I'll touch base with you regularly.

Find a reason to keep in touch. With people you know, ask: Can I put you on my mailing list? We have a wonderful real estate newsletter that keeps you updated on the market, so that you will have the latest in specific real estate information.

Circle Prospecting: Positioning You with a Real Estate Success

Circle prospecting means contacting homeowners in person to provide them with information about a property in their area. The object of circle prospecting is to get a lead.

You should use the circle prospect technique in the following situations:

- A new listing
- A house sold
- A listing sold
- An open house

To use circle prospecting in personal promotion, include this strategy in your listing presentation as a service to sellers and promote yourself as you circle prospect. As a new agent, use this strategy to ask an agent in your office for the opportunity. You have literally 60 to 100 opportunities per month to circle prospect.

There are two important keys to success in circle prospecting:

1. Contact homeowners in person only.
2. Visit the same homeowner three times within a short time.

To prepare for circle prospecting, first decide on the reason why you are calling on the homeowner. Then create your materials, and design your script using the *craft a sales call* (Sales Skill 1) method:

- Introduce yourself, and tell the homeowner why you are there. Be sure to include a benefit (Sales Skill 2) to the homeowner.
- Ask the homeowner about the property: Have you seen it?
- *Ask for a lead* (Sales Skill 3): Do you know anyone who . . . ? (indirect) Are you thinking of . . . ? (direct)

Advanced Technique

Design your script to have a second question ready to follow up the first "no" (see indirect and direct questions). Let's say that your first question is: Do you know anyone who . . .? Your next question can be: Are you thinking of . . .?

It Works

Circle prospecting works for several reasons:

- Homeowners are curious about what is happening in their area.
- Because few agents will take advantage of this opportunity, you have no competition with other agents!
- Homeowners want to see an agent face-to-face.

To increase your chances of a lead, try this advanced technique:

- Familiarity breeds trust—go back three times.

Other Methods for Finding Leads

In the *30 Days to Dollars* plan, three other proactive sources of leads are explained. Immediate sources of leads include: *for-sale-by-owners* (FSBOs) and *expired listings*. A long-term source of leads is: *the geographical farm*.

To select the target markets that you will specialize in: First, assess your background and sales skills. Then, assess your market area. Discuss your market area and your competition for these sources of business with your manager. Your manager is an excellent resource for you as you choose the best target markets on which to focus your efforts.

On the following pages are *contact methods* for developing leads from two of these sources. Because farming is a long-term method of finding leads, it is not included. (See The National Association of REALTORS® magazine, *Real Estate Today*, for excellent articles on farming.) These contact methods are by no means the only ones. Read materials in your office. Find agent specialists in each of these markets. Put together your own "call program."

For-Sale-by-Owners

There are dozens of methods for calling on FSBOs. To successfully contact and convert them, you must make this market a specialty and highly develop your sales approach. Here's an approach that works well for the new agent. Although it requires little developed sales skill, it does require consistency.

The Concept

Surveys show that something happens to FSBOs within six weeks: Owners lists their property, sell it themselves or take it off the market. In your area, do a market survey to determine any differences in time frame for this process and adjust the strategy in Figure 7.1 accordingly.

When executing this program, remember the following important aspects:

Figure 7.1   Converting FSBOs

Call/Time Frame	What To Say	What To Give
When sign first goes up	Introduce yourself; mention saw sign; here are materials to help you; I'll be back	One piece of buying/selling information
Week 2	Same as above; **ask question about materials given***	Same
Week 3	Same	Same
Week 4	Same	Same
Week 5	Same	Same
Week 6	Same	Same

*This question is key to this system.

- Make all sales calls in person.
- Follow up consistently.
- Give a new piece of information (not too much) each week.
- Ask if there is anything about the information you left the prior week that the seller needs help with.
- Don't give detailed information.

By Week Six the sellers will tire of trying to sell their home. When you ask about the information you provided the seller, make an appointment to explain the information while all sellers are present (a first listing appointment). Go to the appointment, and start your listing process.

Success Rate

Using this program, *you can convert one out of five sellers.*

Expired Listings

These sellers want to sell. Your challenge is the dissatisfied customer. Because the home did not sell, the agent who had listed the home has created a high level of customer dissatisfaction. This objection isn't just with that agent and company—it's with all real estate companies. To call on expired listings, you must make this a *specialty* and carefully *plan your strategy.*

You can use any number of ways to contact expired listings. Here are the steps to designing a system:

- Read articles, and find agent specialists in these areas.
- Design your method relative to your market, company and personal style.
- Make the sales calls.
- Make adjustments to your method.

Find the listings that are just expired in your area. Target those that you think will sell if you can get a price reduction. Following is one method successful agents have used to call on expired listings.

Prepare a Script

Hello. I'm Josie Smith of ABC Realty. Is your home still on the market? (If no . . .) Are you still interested in selling it? (If yes . . .) I have some information concerning your home that will be useful to you—whenever or if you decide to put your home back on the market. I assure you I won't ask for a listing now. After all, I don't even know if I could help you until I do some research (e.g., see the home, do a market analysis).

May I come by and drop off this information? (Seller will probably ask you why). It's in all sellers' best interests to move properties, whether real estate agents list and sell the property or not. I want to assist you in your marketing efforts. Hopefully, if in the future you should decide to market your home with a real estate professional, you will feel comfortable enough with me and my service that you will think of me.

Information To Take with You

You want to demonstrate your ability to provide expert information and service that the sellers need to market their property successfully. You should include information in your area about changing market trends, helpful hints to selling and information on why now is the right time to buy.

At the Appointment

Use Sales Skill 5, the "hum" technique, to probe for more illuminating information. Ask these questions:

- So I better understand the specifics of your home, do you mind if I ask you some questions?

- When you sold a home before (if they did), what was the best marketing strategy the agent used?

- In your opinion, why hasn't your home sold?

- If you were to list again, what would you be looking for in a real estate agent?

- Where are you moving to? How soon must you be there?

When you find an area of the seller's need, fill that need with a benefit of your service to the seller. Close for a listing presentation appointment.

Advanced Technique

Go for it! Toward the end of your conversation, when appropriate, ask: What would it take for you to list with me?

Seven Critical Sales Skills for Success

Yes, you can sell homes to people without having effective sales skills. However, it's much more enjoyable for everyone involved if you are a skilled sales communicator. Many buyers have been discouraged from purchasing a home because the salesperson was unskilled at helping the buyer make a buying decision!

Seven Critical Sales Skills

Learning the Seven Critical Sales Skills will help you to develop masterful communication skills that will be useful in any sales situation. Take time to develop these skills. Use them in all sales situations until you're at ease with them. The following skills will save you time, create better relationships and make you more money:

1. *Craft a sales call script.* To get the "biggest bang" from your sales call, always aim for a lead. Refer to "How To Craft a Sales Call" in Section 7 for suggestions on how to call on people you know. This same crafting method can be used in designing any sales call. This sales skill is practiced and applied in Week One. (See page 119 for more information on how to craft a sales call.)

2. *Attach benefits.* Show the customer that there is something in it for him. Too often, salespeople only think of what a sale will do for them, not what it will provide for the buyers of their services! This sales skill is practiced and applied in Week One and is demonstrated on the audiotape. (See page 121 for more information on how to attach benefits.)

3. *Ask a question to get the order.* This sales skill is introduced in Section 7, when you're crafting a sales call to a person you know, and when you're circle prospecting. It seems simplistic, but too often salespeople fail to ask for the order. To ensure that you get a lead, craft and apply this simple yet critical sales skill in all sales situations. This sale skill is introduced in Week One and is demonstrated on the audiotape. (See page 121 for more information on how to ask for a lead.

4. *Use the AAA method of objection-busting.* This method of crafting a process to counter, defuse or anticipate objections is critical to each sales situation. In truth, all salespeople encounter objections and rejections with each sales call. With the AAA method, you learn to craft a whole process that takes objections from an adversary relationship to a discussion. Use this method, introduced in Week Two and demonstrated on the audiotape, to qualify buyers and sellers, and throughout the entire sales cycle. (See page 122 for information on crafting an objection-buster using the AAA method.)

5. *Use the "hum" technique.* This technique is a simplified version of asking questions that encourage the buyer of your services to open up (in sales, these are called *open-ended questions*). This method also helps you get in-depth information so that you understand your buyer's needs (in sales, this is called *probing*). Use this technique, introduced in Week Three and demonstrated on the audiotape in all sales situations to help you be a good *listener*. (See page 124 for more information on crafting the "hum" technique.

6. *Tie down your benefit statement.* Sometimes agents get enamored with the sound of their own sales voices. The "tie-down" brings the buyer of your services back into the conversation, and allows you to check to be sure you are still on track. This sales skill is introduced

in Week Four and demonstrated on the audiotape. Use it throughout the sales cycle to ensure that the buyer of your services is still buying what you have to sell. (See the information on page 125 about how to craft a "tie down.")

7. ***Discover the motive that drives the buyers' decisions.*** People make decisions based on feelings and rationalize these decisions with facts. For example, let's say your friend buys a Mercedes. Does he say that he bought it because he wants status? No. He says he bought it because studies show the car will actually cost less in the long run because it will hold its value. While this may be true, your friend's desire for status prompted his decision. (Emotions drive decisions.)

Using this sales skill, you can discover the dominant motive of the buyer of services. Then, you can create a meaningful sales cycle to appeal to that particular buyer of services. To close, you remind the buyer of his or her motive. This sales skill is introduced in Week Four and demonstrated on the audiotape. Use it throughout the sales cycle to help the buyer of services to motivate himself or herself to make a good buying decision. (See the information on page 126 about how to discover the "dominant buying motive.")

Sales Skill 1: How To Craft a Sales Call

The following method of crafting calls works for crafting any initial sales call. Since this is a prospecting method and a sales skill, I have included it in Sections 7 and 8. Use the worksheet in Figure 8.1 to craft a sales call. Here's the process:

- Think of a particular person to call.
- Determine potential real estate needs and *benefits* to this person that you can provide.
- To discover these needs, write three questions to ask this person.
- Determine your *call objective.*
- Write a question to *get a lead* or appointment—meet your objective.
- Write an opening statement.

Example

- The person: Joe Smith, a friend of your family.
- A potential real estate need and benefit to Joe is a rental home, which will reduce his tax burden.

- Three questions to ask:
    1. Is the equity in your present home enough to get a second mortgage to refinance for money to buy another home?
    2. Have you considered reducing your tax burden?
    3. Have you looked into purchasing a home as a rental?
- The call objective is to get an appointment.
- The question to get an appointment: When can we explore this potential?
- The opening statement is: I've been thinking about you. I'm in real estate now. I'm exploring how to help people ease financial burdens with real estate.

Figure 8.1   Craft Your Own Sales Call

Name of person:_____

Potential real estate need:_____

Benefit to the person of
your service:_____

Three questions:
    1. _____

    2. _____

    3. _____

Your call objective:_____

Question to get the order:_____

Opening statement:_____

Practice this sales call with a friend until you are comfortable.

Sales Skill 2: Attach a Benefit

A *benefit* is a statement to the buyer of your services that answers the question in the buyer's mind: What does it mean to me?

Too often a salesperson recites the facts (called *features* in sales), thinking that, if those facts are important to the salesperson, they must be important to the buyer. Unfortunately, this is not generally the case. What is important and interesting to the buyer is how he or she can use these facts. A three-car garage is a benefit to the person who owns three cars (or lots of things). It's merely an unwanted expense to a single person with one car!

How do you discover what is important to a buyer? When a buyer requests a specific feature or need (e.g., a large family room), ask *why*? Then, when you show a home with a large family room, remind the buyer that *it provides plenty of space for that growing family*. In this way the buyer sees the relevance to the large family room.

Following is an example of a benefit-attached statement: The home has a *two-car garage* (feature), so that *you can park your two full-sized cars there* (benefit). Benefits answer the buyer's question: So what? To attach benefits to features, state the feature first. Then, "bridge" to the benefit with the words "so that . . . ."

Practice attaching benefits to the following features:

Feature	Bridge	Benefit
Family room . . .	so that . . .	
Fireplace . . .	so that . . .	
Low house payments . . .	so that . . .	

Referrals to the agent are a benefit to the referring source because . . .

Listing with me is a benefit to you, the seller, because . . .

Working with me to find a home is a benefit to you, the buyer, because . . .

Sales Skill 3: Ask a Question To Get the Order

What is an order? A lead, a buying decision, a "yes" of any type. Usually, an order is given to an agent in reply to a question asked by the agent.

Do buyers give REALTORS® leads without being asked? It depends on the level of trust and rapport between agent and buyer.

Why take chances? In this overcommunicated world, it's hard for any of us to find the energy to ask the salesperson to sell us something! Also, with a big-ticket item like a home, buyers may be less apt to do the salesperson's work! You should always *ask a question to get an order*. Successful salespeople always ask. Less successful salespeople are afraid to ask—and may miss golden opportunities to increase their businesses.

Many agents expect customers to tell the agent that they want to buy a property. So, the agent waits for the customers to give an indication that they are ready to buy. In most cases, customers will not ask to buy. Once in a while, they will.

Asking for a Specific Order—A Lead

To get a lead, attach a benefit to your question. For example: Well, Sally, I appreciate your telling me that you would help me get started in real estate. When you give me names of people who want to buy or sell real estate, *you'll be helping your friends get the very best service available* (benefit). The only way to become proficient at asking for leads is: practice.

Getting Leads When Knocking on Doors

When knocking on doors, you can phrase a question two ways:

1. Direct question: Are you thinking of selling/buying?
2. Indirect question: Do you know of anyone who is thinking of buying/selling?

Sales Skill 4: AAA Method of Objection-Busting

Just think of objections as one of the six "no's" that you need to accept from your buyer to get to "yes."

To gracefully craft an objection-buster, use the **AAA** method:

- Agree
- Ask
- Answer

When the objection comes from the buyer (the buyer of your services, whether a purchaser or seller), *agree* that he or she has an important point. After all, it's important to the buyer! Instead of countering the objection and risking an argument, *ask* more questions to discover just exactly what the buyer is talking about. *Answer* the objection with new information. Then, close!!

Figure 8.2   Crafting an Objection-Buster

Objection _____

    You **Agree** _____

    You **Ask** _____

More Probing Questions

    (Tell me more.) _____

    (Please explain.) _____

    (Then what happened.) _____

    (How, what, when, why, how much. . . .) _____

    _____

You **Answer**

    (Use visuals.) _____

    _____

    _____

Close

_____

_____

_____

_____

The dialogue would go something like this:

Buyer: I want to wait to purchase. (objection)

You agree: I understand your concern. Buying is a big decision.

You ask: To help me understand exactly what you're thinking about, do you mind if I ask you a few questions?

You probe and ask more: Tell me more about waiting to purchase.

You provide an answer: There's some information that could help you make the best decision. Let me show you. . . . Do you have any questions? Let's go ahead.

Use the worksheet, Crafting an Objection-Buster (see Figure 8.2), to create an objection-buster for each of the objections you are working on in *Up and Running*.

Sales Skill 5: The "Hum" Technique

Often agents assume that they know what buyers mean by the words they use and jump ahead, many times missing important clues. For example, a buyer says he wants a *deal*. You assume you know what *deal* means to the buyer, and you show him homes that may not be deals to the buyer.

To avoid jumping to conclusions, use the *hum technique*. This skill, a simplified version of the question-and-probing sales skill, is fun to use. It provides lots of information and encourages the buyer to keep talking.

Here's the technique:

- Ask an open-ended question (one that requires more of an answer than yes or no). Hint: Open-ended questions are those that start with who, what, when, where, how much, why.

- Listen to the answer, pick out a core word and repeat the word back to the talker, using a questioning upswing to your word. This will encourage your questioner to tell you more.

- As your talker talks, simply *hum*. This, too, will encourage the buyer to continue talking. You'll discover lots of information and show that you are a skilled, attentive listener.

The dialogue would go something like this:

Buyer says: I want a deal.

You ask: Deal?

Buyer explains. You hum, encouraging the buyer to give you more information. Alternate saying key words with hums.

When To Use This Sales Skill

Use this skill all the time. Successful salespeople aren't good talkers; they're good listeners. See how long you can continue a conversation without actually saying a whole sentence. When you can talk with someone for three minutes and let them do all the talking, you're on your way to becoming an effective salesperson.

Sales Skill 6: Tying Down Your Benefit

This is another simple sales skill, but one that's very important for creating rapport, agreement and movement toward closing. To use this technique, attach a question to your benefit statement. This ties down the benefit in your customer's mind. It relates the benefit to the buyer.

For example: This home has a three-car garage, which allows you to keep your antique cars at home, saving you rent. *That is what you want, isn't it?*

Practice tie-downs using the worksheet in Figure 8.3.

Figure 8.3   Practice Tie-Downs

Feature	Bridge	Benefit	Tie-down question
Large lot	so that. . .	you can have. . .	That's what you want, isn't it?
Private setting			
Quiet street			
Low down payment			

Sales Skill 7: Discover the Motive That Drives the Decision

As a salesperson, you need to have an attitude like Detective Colombo. Always wearing an old raincoat, Colombo spent his time trying to discover people's motives for the crimes he investigated. Without a motive, Colombo couldn't figure out who did it.

What are motives? They are emotional reasons that people take actions.

Why do people buy homes? To fill emotional needs—motives. Three bathrooms are not very motivating; however, providing space for a growing family is. To find motives, attach benefits to features. Benefits lead to dominant buying motives, the main emotional reasons behind people make buying decisions. Buying motives include:

- Personal space
- Prestige
- Security
- Family security

One motive always dominates the others. People often do not know their own dominant buying motives, but they can express their needs in terms of features. They can agree on benefits. You need to help them translate their physical needs to emotional needs.

How can you identify which needs people are trying to fill? By the benefits they want to have as they buy or sell. For example: "I want a nice home for my family, on a safe cul-de-sac." The dominant buying motive is obviously family security.

Why did you buy your last home? Identify *your* own emotional needs. Your success in selling homes to people depends on your ability to discover dominant buying motives and to remind buyers of these motives as you work with and ask them closing questions. Your success in listing homes at the right price depends on your ability to help identify sellers' dominant buying motives, to help them motivate themselves to sell.

When you're sleuthing for dominant buying motives, use the worksheet shown in Figure 8.4.

Figure 8.4   Dominant Buying Motives

Features They Want	Benefits to Them	Dominant Buying Motive

Sellers and Buyers

Figure 9.1   For Sellers: Qualified Listing Appointments

Date of Presentation	Name	Address	Want To Sell	Both Home	2 Hours Pre-Scheduled	How Much $ Want	Marketing Presentation Completed	Results

Figure 9.2   Evaluate Property Salability

1. Property listed at competitive price.   Yes____   No____

2. Full-term listing agreement.   Yes____   No____

3. Seller to complete obvious repairs/cleaning
   prior to showing.   Yes____   No____

4. Easy access (e.g., key, phone for showing).   Yes____   No____

5. Yard sign.   Yes____   No____

6. Immediate possession.   Yes____   No____

7. Extras included (e.g., appliances).   Yes____   No____

8. Available for first tour.   Yes____   No____

9. Government terms available.   Yes____   No____

10. Owner financing available.   Yes____   No____

11. Below market down payment.   Yes____   No____

12. Below market interest rate.   Yes____   No____

13. Post-dated price reduction.   Yes____   No____

14. Market commission.   Yes____   No____

15. In my evaluation, this property will sell within
    listed market range, in normal market time
    for this area.   Yes____   No____

16. My credibility as a professional will be
    enhanced by listing this property.   Yes____   No____

Figure 9.3 Qualified Buyers

Date of Qualify Meeting	Name	Address	Qualify Checklist Used	Both @ Qualifying Session	# Showings	Sales

Figure 9.4   Evaluate Your Customer's Potential

Rate on a scale of 1–4 (4 being the highest)

1. Customer is motivated to purchase. (Rate each spouse/partner separately.)	1	2	3	4
2. Customer is realistic about price range expectations.	1	2	3	4
3. Customer is open and cooperative.	1	2	3	4
4. Customer will purchase in a timely manner.	1	2	3	4
5. Customer is a referral source and will provide referrals.	1	2	3	4
6. Customer has agreed that you will be his or her exclusive agent.	1	2	3	4
7. Agent has established a positive rapport with customer.	1	2	3	4
8. Customer will meet with loan officer.	1	2	3	4
9. Customer answered financial questions openly.	1	2	3	4
10. Customer has no other agent obligations.	1	2	3	4
11. If customer has home to sell, he or she is realistic about price.	1	2	3	4
12. Customer will devote sufficient time to purchasing process.	1	2	3	4
13. Both spouses/partners will be available to look for home.	1	2	3	4

Is this customer worthy of your time, energy and expertise?

Walking Through a Sample Business Plan

Figure 10.1   Joan's Yearly Goals Translated to Monthly Goals and Activities

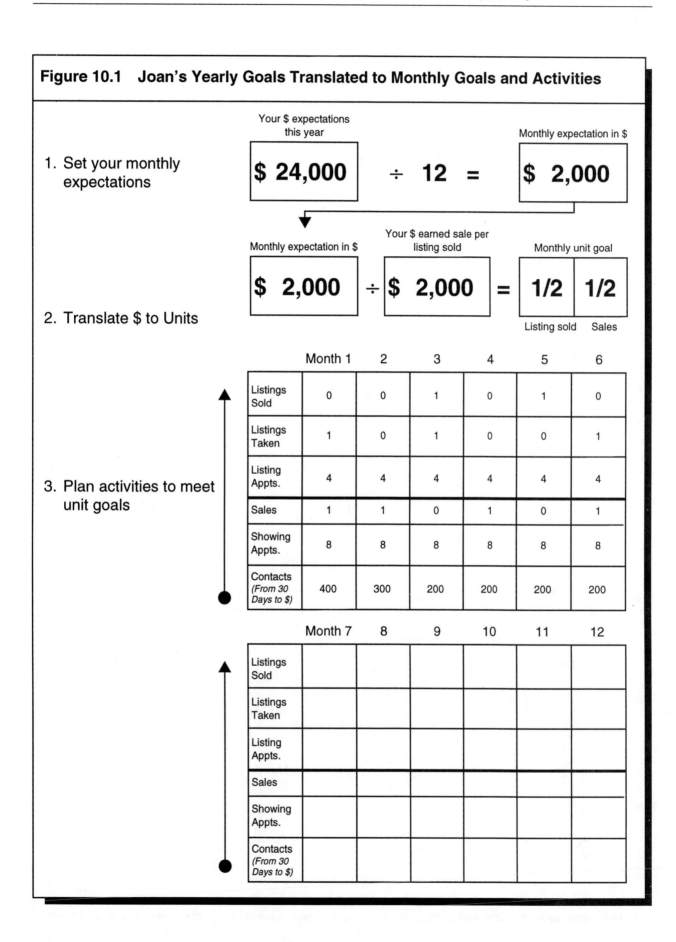

Figure 10.2   Joan's Plan: From Breakeven to Profitability

1. Estimate your activities and when they will create income. Start with face-to-face contacts.

Activity / Income	1	2	3	4	5	6	7	8	9	10	11	12	Totals
Closings*		1	1	1		1							
Sales*	1	1		1	1	1							
Listings sold*			1		1	1							
Listings secured	1		1		1								
Showings	8	8	8	8	8	8							
Listing presentations	4	4	4	4	4	4							
Face-to-face contacts	400	300	200	200	200	200							

*Each unit is worth $2,000 in commissions earned or paid.

2. Tally your expenses per month. Log in your projected earnings and "paids."

	1	2	3	4	5	6	7	8	9	10	11	12	Totals
Business expenses†	1,149	748	818	748	888	818							
Earned income†	2,000	2,000	0	2,000	2,000	4,000							
Paid income	0	0	2,000	2,000	0	2,000							

	1	2	3	4	5	6	7	8	9	10	11	12	Totals
Profit per month	-$1,149	-$748	$1,182	$1,252	-$888	$1,182							

†See *The Real Estate Agent's Business Planning Guide* for a detailed listing of expenses and budgeting.

Figure 10.3 Joan's First Week: 30 Days to Dollars

Activity	Weekly Minimum
1. Contact people you know/meet.	
In-person calls	20
Phone calls	30
Follow-up mailers sent	50
Joan contacts 50 people.	
2. Circle prospect in person.	25
Joan circle prospects 25 homes.	
3. Choose one additional activity from these.	
Farm Area in-person contacts	50
or	
FSBOs in-person or phone contacts	25
or	
Expired listings in-person or phone contacts	25
4. Hold public open houses.	1
Joan holds 1 open house.	

Total weekly minimuim in-person/phone contacts: **100-125**

Figure 10.4   Joan's Second Week: 30 Days to Dollars

Activity	Weekly Minimum
1. Contact people you know/meet.	
In-person calls	20
Phone calls	30
Follow-up mailers sent	50
Joan contacts 50 people.	
2. Circle prospect in person.	25
Joan circle prospects 25 homes.	
3. Choose one additional activity from these.	
Farm Area — in-person contacts	50
or	
FSBOs — in-person or phone contacts	25
or	
Expired listings — in-person or phone contacts	25
Joan calls on 25 expired listings.	
4. Hold public open houses.	1
Joan holds 1 open house.	

Total weekly minimuim in-person/phone contacts: 100-125

Figure 10.5   Joan's Third Week: 30 Days to Dollars

Activity	Weekly Minimum
1. Contact people you know/meet.	
In-person calls	20
Phone calls	30
Follow-up mailers sent	50
Joan contacts 50 people.	
2. Circle prospect in person.	25
Joan circle prospects 25 homes.	
3. Choose one additional activity from these.	
Farm Area in-person contacts	50
or	
FSBOs in-person or phone contacts	25
or	
Expired listings in-person or phone contacts	25
Joan calls on 25 FSBOs and 25 expireds.	
4. Hold public open houses.	1
Joan holds 1 open house.	

Total weekly minimuim in-person/phone contacts: 100-125

Figure 10.6   Joan's Fourth Week: 30 Days to Dollars

Activity	Weekly Minimum
1. Contact people you know/meet.	
In-person calls	20
Phone calls	30
Follow-up mailers sent	50
Joan contacts 50 people.	
2. Circle prospect in person.	25
Joan circle prospects 25 homes.	
3. Choose one additional activity from these.	
Farm Area in-person contacts	50
or	
FSBOs in-person or phone contacts	25
or	
Expired listings in-person or phone contacts	25
Joan calls on 25 FSBOs and 25 expireds.	
4. Hold public open houses.	1
Joan holds 1 open house.	

Total weekly minimuim in-person/phone contacts: **100-125**

Figure 10.7   Joan's 30 Days to Dollars Plan (Prospecting)

Month: _____

Proactive Activities

	Week 1 G	Week 1 A	Week 2 G	Week 2 A	Week 3 G	Week 3 A	Week 4 G	Week 4 A	Totals G	Totals A
People you know/meet [50/week]	50	50	50	50	50	50	50	50	200	200
Circle prospect [25/week]	25	25	25	25	25	25	25	25	100	100
Farm [50/week]	0	0	0	0	0	0	0	0	0	0
FSBOs [25/week]	0	0	0	0	25	25	25	25	50	50
Expireds [25/week]	0	0	25	25	25	25	25	25	75	75

Reactive Activities

	Week 1 G	Week 1 A	Week 2 G	Week 2 A	Week 3 G	Week 3 A	Week 4 G	Week 4 A	Totals G	Totals A
Open houses [1min]	1	1	1	1	1	1	1	1	4	4

G=Goals
A=Actuals

Proactive means you go out and find a prospect.
Reactive means you wait for a prospect to come to you.

Figure 10.8 Joan's Monthly Activity Scorecard

Month: _____

Buyer Activities

	Week 1		Week 2		Week 3		Week 4		Totals	
	G	A	G	A	G	A	G	A	G	A
Counseling Appointments w/ buyers	2	2	2	2	2	2	2	2	8	8
Qualified buyer showings	2	2	2	2	2	2	2	2	8	8
# sales							1	1	1	1

Listing Activities

	Week 1		Week 2		Week 3		Week 4		Totals	
	G	A	G	A	G	A	G	A	G	A
Qualified listing appointments	1	1	1	1	1	1	1	1	4	4
Marketable listings secured	0	0	0	0	1	1	0	0	1	1
# of listings sold	0	0	0	0	0	0	0	0	0	0

G=Goals   A=Actuals

Figure 10.9 Joan's Weekly Plan

Week: One   Name: Joan Smith

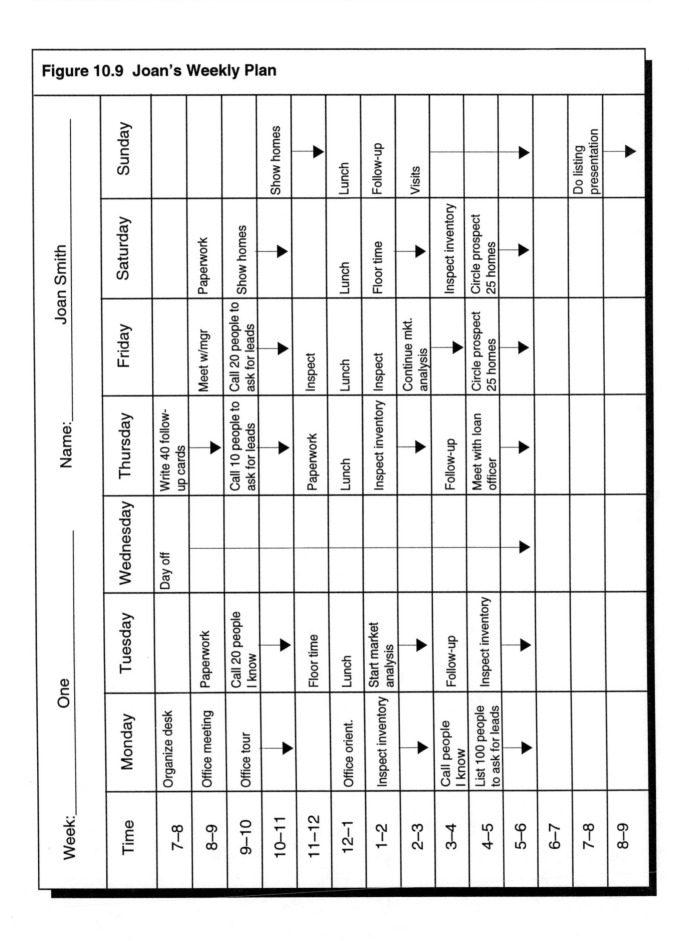

Time	Monday	Tuesday	Wednesday	Thursday	Friday	Saturday	Sunday
7–8	Organize desk		Day off	Write 40 follow-up cards			
8–9	Office meeting	Paperwork			Meet w/mgr	Paperwork	
9–10	Office tour	Call 20 people I know		Call 10 people to ask for leads	Call 20 people to ask for leads	Show homes	Show homes
10–11	→	→		→	→	→	
11–12		Floor time		Paperwork	Inspect		→
12–1	Office orient.	Lunch		Lunch	Lunch	Lunch	Lunch
1–2	Inspect inventory	Start market analysis		Inspect inventory	Inspect	Floor time	Follow-up
2–3	→	→		→	Continue mkt. analysis	→	Visits
3–4	Call people I know	Follow-up		Follow-up	→	Inspect inventory	
4–5	List 100 people to ask for leads	Inspect inventory		Meet with loan officer	Circle prospect 25 homes	Circle prospect 25 homes	→
5–6	→	→	→	→	→	→	
6–7							
7–8							Do listing presentation
8–9							→

Forms To Create Your Own Plan

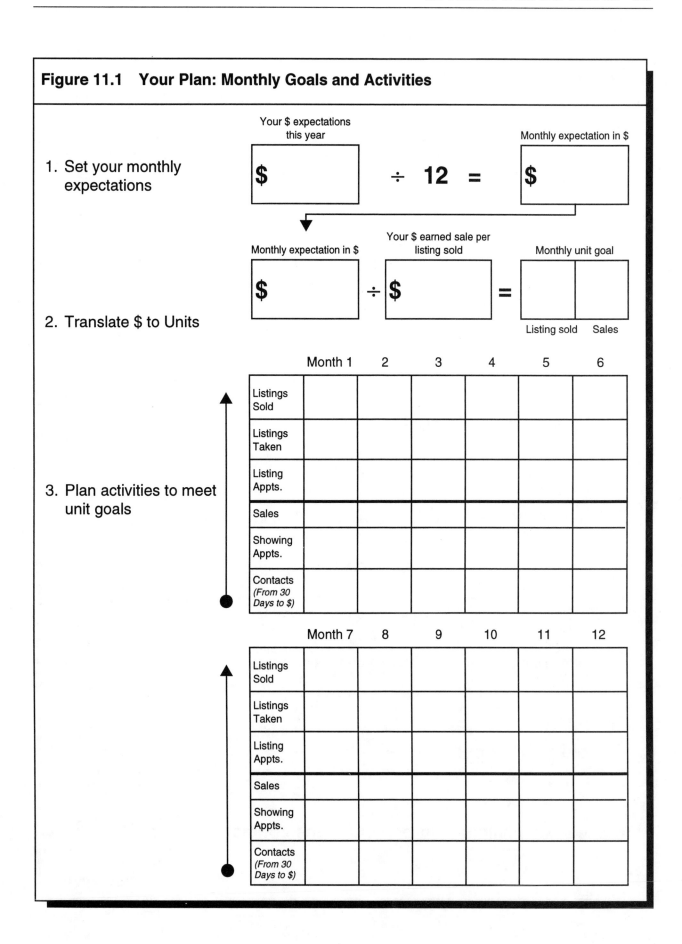

Figure 11.1 Your Plan: Monthly Goals and Activities

Figure 11.2   30 Days to Dollars

Activity	Weekly Minimum
1. Contact people you know/meet.	
In-person calls	20
Phone calls	30
Follow-up mailers sent	50
2. Circle prospect in person.	25
3. Choose one additional activity from these.	
Farm Area in-person contacts	50
or	
FSBOs in-person or phone contacts	25
or	
Expired listings in-person or phone contacts	25
4. Hold public open houses.	1

Total weekly minimuim in-person/phone contacts: **100-125**

Figure 11.3   Your 30 Days to Dollars Plan (Prospecting)

Month: _____

Proactive Activities	Week 1		Week 2		Week 3		Week 4		Totals	
	G	A	G	A	G	A	G	A	G	A
People you know/meet [50/week]										
Circle prospect [25/week]										
Farm [50/week]										
FSBOs [25/week]										
Expireds [25/week]										
Reactive Activities										
Open houses [1min]										

G=Goals
A=Actuals

Proactive means you go out and find a prospect.
Reactive means you wait for a prospect to come to you.

Figure 11.4   Your Monthly Activity Scorecard

Month: _____

Buyer Activities

	Week 1		Week 2		Week 3		Week 4		Totals	
	G	A	G	A	G	A	G	A	G	A
Counseling Appointments w / buyers										
Qualified buyer showings										
# sales										

Listing Activities

	Week 1		Week 2		Week 3		Week 4		Totals	
	G	A	G	A	G	A	G	A	G	A
Qualified listing appointments										
Marketable listings secured										
# of listings sold										

G=Goals   A=Actuals

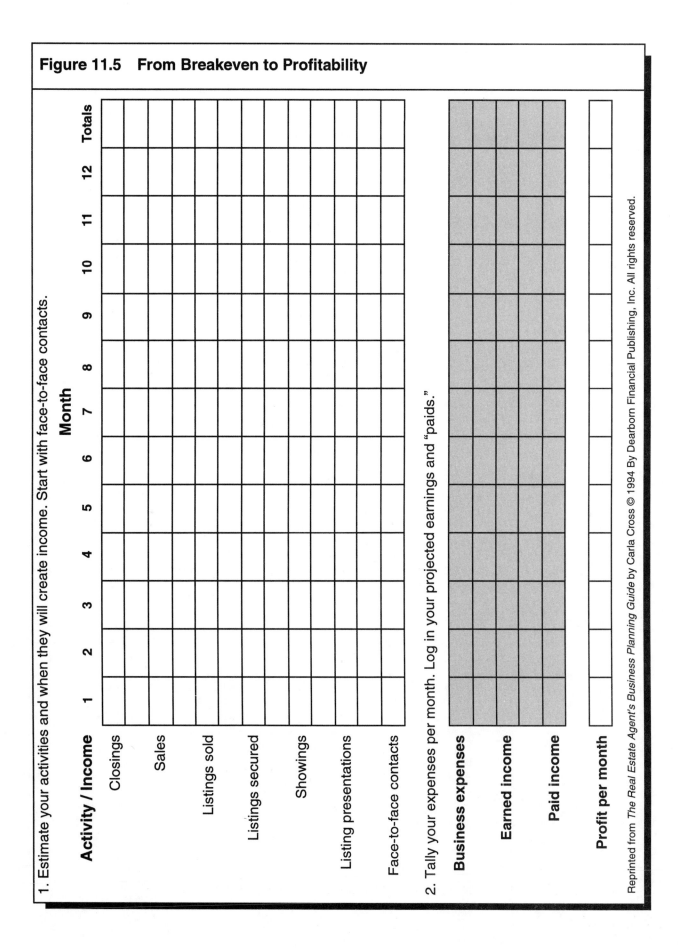

Figure 11.5   From Breakeven to Profitability

References

Reaching Your Career Objectives

How about a Career in Real Estate? Carla Cross. Chicago: Real Estate Education Company, a division of Dearborn Financial Publishing, Inc., 1993. Endorsed and recommended by the Real Estate Brokerage Managers' Council.

How To Create a Professional Portfolio That Sells You. Carla Cross Seminars, 1995. Includes full instructions and audiotape. Carla Cross Seminars, 1070 Idylwood Dr. S.W., Issaquah, WA 98027. 206-392-6914/1-800-296-2599.

List the Buyer System, 1994. Carla Cross Seminars. Includes 24-page buyer's guide plus insider tips on how to control buyers and get loyalty for life. Carla Cross Seminars, 1070 Idylwood Dr. S.W., Issaquah, WA 98027. 206-392-6914/1-800-296-2599.

The Real Estate Agent's Business Planning Guide. Carla Cross. Chicago: Real Estate Education Company, a division of Dearborn Financial Publishing, Inc., 1994. Endorsed and recommended by the Real Estate Brokerage Managers' Council.

The Recruiter. Carla Cross Seminars, 1992. The manager's personal recruiting presentation, with complete instructions on how to assemble and how to use to recruit. Two audiotapes and two-color presentation materials. Carla Cross Seminars, 1070 Idylwood Dr. S.W., Issaquah, WA 98027. 206-392-6914/1-800-296-2599. Endorsed and recommended by the Real Estate Brokerage Managers' Council.

Assistance for Managers, Trainers and Mentors

The Conative Connection. Kathy Kolbe. New York: Addison-Wesley Publishing Co., Inc., 1990.

"Crosscoaching": A Proven Mentor Program. Carla Cross Seminars, 1995. Critical points for effective mentor programs. Specific mentor and new agent guides, how to train, manage mentors. Detailed, ready to use, field-tested and proven. Includes audiotapes to explain program, save manager's time. Carla Cross Seminars, 1070 Idylwood Dr. S.W., Issaquah, WA 98027. 206-392-6914/1-800-296-2599.

Index